CONCEPT AND OBJECT

CONCEPT AND OBJECT

The Unity of the Proposition in Logic and Psychology

by
ANTHONY PALMER

ROUTLEDGE

LONDON AND NEW YORK

First published in 1988 by
Routledge
11 New Fetter Lane, London EC4P 4EE
Published in the USA by
Routledge
in association with Methuen Inc.
29 West Street, New York, NY 10001

Set in 10/12 Baskerville
by Butler and Tanner
and printed in Great Britain
by Butler and Tanner Ltd
Frome and London

Library of Congress Cataloging in Publication Data
Palmer, Anthony.
Concept and object.
(Studies in philosophical psychology)
Bibliography: p.
Includes index.
1. Proposition (logic)   History   20th century.
I. Title.   II. Series.
BC181.P35 1988   160   87-24342
ISBN 0-415-00172-2

FOR JEAN

In the nature of the case some things have perceptible likenesses which are easy to grasp, and which can be readily shown to an enquirer, when he asks to have things explained and you want an easy way of pointing them out without the trouble of explaining. But with the greatest and most valuable things this is not so. These have no image clearly made for men which you can display to your enquirer and bring within the range of his senses so as to give any tolerable satisfaction to his mind. That is why we must practice the ability to give and to follow explanations of anything whatever. For it is by explanation and by nothing else that the non-bodily things, the finest and the greatest, are plainly displayed: and all we are now saying is said for the sake of these.

THE ELEATIC STRANGER

CONTENTS

ACKNOWLEDGMENTS

Much of what I have written has its origins in conversation with Gilbert Ryle in the last five years years of his life. Although in chapter five I have been highly critical of his views it should be clear how much I am indebted to him. It also owes a great deal to conversations over the years with Guy Robinson.

I have made extensive use of some of my previously published papers. These are:

'Parasites Cut Loose' in *Idealism Past and Present*, Royal Institute of Philosophy Lecture Series 13, ed. Godfrey Vesey, Cambridge University Press, 1982.

'Ryle *Cogitans*' in *Philosophy*, 1984.

'A Meeting of Minds' in *Mind*, 1984.

'The Limits of A.I.' in *The Mind and the Machine* ed. S. Torrance, Ellis Horwood, 1984.

'Cognitivism and Computer Simulation' in *Cognitive Psychology in Question*, ed. Alan Costal and Arthur Still, Harvester Press, 1987

I am grateful to the editor of *Mind*, the editor of *Philosophy*, The Royal Institute of Philosophy, Alan Costal, Arthur Still, S. Torrance, Harvester Press, Cambridge University Press, and Ellis Horwood for allowing me to use this material again.

PREFACE

What is presented in this book is an account of the most distinctive and influential responses by twentieth century philosophers to a problem which, although it is as old as Plato, is sometimes called Bradley's problem. The simplest way to characterise it is to use Russell's words from *The Principles of Mathematics*. 'A proposition ... is essentially a unity and when analysis has destroyed the unity, no enumeration of constituents will restore the proposition.' If this is true, what kind of account of the analysis of propositions can be given? My general contention is that an examination of the various responses to this problem shows that the now widely held view that we are on the verge of a theory of meaning which will form the basis of an assault upon the perennial problems of philosophy is mistaken. The pursuit of such a theory is the pursuit of a chimera.

In the first chapter I try to show how the problem became central in twentieth century philosophy as a result of the depsychologising of logic brought about by the work of Bradley and Frege. In the second I explore Russell's struggles with it in the first part of *The Principles of Mathematics* where the idea of 'denoting', used by him in a technical sense, is introduced to solve the problem. I try to show how this idea in its turn led Russell, *via* the notion of a propositional function, to his account of the variable deployed in his famous paper 'On Denoting' which he thought enabled him to dispense with his technical sense of the word. I argue that Frege showed this account of the variable to be incoherent.

Frege's own response to the problem in which the distinction between concept and object is fundamental is dealt with in the third chapter. As against the view given currency in Michael Dummett's writings that the problem does indeed have a technical or theoretical solution I argue that the upshot of Frege's work was the conclusion that the problem has no such solution, with all that this implies for the project of a theory of meaning or the idea of philosophy of language as First Philosophy.

Chapter four is concerned with the bearing of Wittgenstein's *Tractatus Logico Philosophicus* on the idea of propositional constituents. Despite the fact that many of the defects in Russell's introduction to it have long been recognised, nevertheless, from the point of view of this problem it continues to be read in Russell's way. Yet what Wittgenstein says about objects, symbols, variables and the general form of a proposition cannot be given a Russellian interpretation. I argue that when we take seriously what Wittgenstein says about these we must conclude that the idea of propositional constituents which generates Bradley's problem, together with the conception of logical form which goes with it, has to be rejected; and that Wittgenstein did in fact reject it.

After speaking of the *Tractatus* I turn to Ryle, for although he himself did not refer to the problem in that way it is remarkable how much of his work begins from a consideration of Bradley's problem. The work of Frege and Wittgenstein's *Tractatus* had persuaded him of the importance of the distinction between concepts and objects with its consequence that concepts cannot be made into the subjects of true (or false) propositions. However, like Russell, and unlike Frege and Wittgenstein, Ryle continued to think that the problem required a theoretical solution. In chapter five I try to bring out how, in pursuit of such a solution, he sought to give the ideal of conceptual investigations a linguistic turn. Ryle thought that truths about linguistic items, provided they were the right kind of truths, could give us indirectly truths about concepts. I try to bring out why this cannot be done.

If the book were to keep to chronological order chapter six would have been about Wittgenstein's continued response to the problem in his later work. This, however, is reserved for chapter seven. Chapter six is given over to a consideration of the work of Donald Davidson. The reason for this is that if what I have to say about it is correct Davidson's work has more in common with that of Russell and Ryle, from the point of view of Bradley's problem, than it has with that of Frege and Witt-genstein. Like Russell's technical sense of 'denoting' and Ryle's special kind of truths about linguistic items, Davidson's holism, i.e. his extension of Frege's context principle from sentences to language, is designed primarily to secure a theoretical solution to the problem of propositional constituents and the related notion of logical form. I argue that considerations about the nature of truth work against the idea that a theory of truth can provide a theory of meaning in the way in which Davidson suggests.

Wittgenstein had already in the *Tractatus* rejected theoretical solutions to the problem of propositional constituents. In the *Philosophical Investigations* he developed a quite new conception of conceptual investigations. One effect of Davidson's work has been to distract attention from the importance of this concep-tion. In chapter seven I use Wittgenstein's remarks on Frazer's *Golden Bough* and his *On Certainty* to show how the importance he attached to agreement in judgments bears on Bradley's problem. The view I advocate involves a rejection of the reading of the *Investigations* which has been developed by Saul Kripke.

Since the problem with which the book is concerned arose in this century as a result of the depsychologising of logic I turn in the last two chapters to the way in which our attitude to it affects the way in which we think about the nature of the mind. In chapter eight I argue that Strawson's influential account of the concept of a person is based upon the view about the make-up of propositions which bears a remarkable resemblance to

the views of Russell in the *Principles*, which Frege had already
provided powerful reasons for rejecting. I argue that defects
in Strawson's account of propositions generate corresponding
defects in his account of the concept of a person. In the final
chapter I argue that similar defects infect the increasingly widely
held belief that work in the field of artificial intelligence and
computer simulation is likely to solve problems in the philosophy
of mind. The new 'way of ideas' as defended, for example, by a
philosopher such as Daniel Dennett has all the disadvantages of
the old together with the further disadvantage that it makes us
lose sight of the gains in philosophical understanding which
arose from the depsychologising of logic.

ONE

THE DEPSYCHOLOGISING OF LOGIC

It was customary for Oxford philosophers of the mid-twentieth century, at the peak of their influence, to see the watershed of their development in the depsychologising of logic and therefore of philosophy associated with the names of Bradley and Frege. Gilbert Ryle, in the introduction he wrote for a series of third programme talks under the title of *The Revolution in Philosophy*, published in 1956, both took himself to be, and can be taken as, representative of such a view. What impressed him about Bradley and Frege was that:

> Both were in revolt against 'psychologism', in revolt, that is, against one dominant element in the teaching of John Stuart Mill. Mill, transmitting the legacy of Hume, had tended to treat problems of logic and epistemology as problems to be solved by associationist psychology. Frege and Bradley in different ways and with different emphasis distinguished sharply between psychology on the one side and philosophy and logic on the other; the ideas, impressions and feelings that were the subject matter of psychology and whatever it was that formed the subject matters of philosophy and logic (Ryle, 1956, p. 6).

It is not difficult to see why Ryle thought this a turning point. The Cartesian dualism of mind and body was a stalking horse for him from very early on in his career. To show that Descartes' *ideas* were irrelevant to logical concerns was, from his point of view, the important first step towards the acknowledgement that there are in fact no concerns whatsoever to which they are relevant. Ryle himself, seven years before, had used a depsychologised conception of logic and philosophy to castigate Descartes' views as the myth of the ghost in the machine. Moreover his anti-Cartesian impetus seemed to harmonise well with Wittgenstein's arguments, posthumously published only three years earlier in the *Philosophical Investigations*, against the possibility of an essentially private language, which is how any language would have to be seen from within Descartes' philosophy. From this anti-Cartesian perspective the differences between Bradley and Frege could seem like minor variations in a large scale philosophical shift. The differences between the two philosophers are, however, highly significant.

Bradley's anti-psychologism arose directly from considerations about the nature of judgment; considerations which led him to question the idea that logic has a propriety subject matter, and ultimately generated in him a scepticism about logic and reasoning in general. Frege's anti-psychologism, on the other hand, was originally independent of such considerations. For him the depsychologising of logic was accomplished independently of his undoubtedly important and influential views about judgments and their contents, and was accompanied by a firm view of the subject matter of logic. Their anti-psychologism apart, it is hard to over-emphasise the differences between Bradley and Frege.

Bradley

When Bradley and Frege were writing the dualism of mind and body was still entrenched. It is important to realise that both of them subscribed to it. Neither seems ever to have been in any doubt that there are both minds and bodies; both mental entities and physical entities. Indeed the depsychologising of logic which both of them advocated required that they did, for it was essentially the relevance of Cartesian ideas to logic that they called into question.

At first sight, however, Ryle's reference to Mill does not seem to be accurate. In his *System of Logic* Mill had developed the view that a proposition is made up of names, and he argued that these names should not be construed as the names of ideas but as the names of things, which seems to be a straightforward contradiction of Ryle's claim. Mill maintained that 'When I say that "the sun is the cause of the day", I do not mean that my idea of the sun causes or excites in me the idea of day' but that 'a certain physical fact which is caused by the sun's presence ... causes another physical fact which is called day' and he stated explicitly that names shall 'always be spoken of in this work as names of things and not merely of our ideas of things' (Mill, 1843, p. 15). He then proceeded to introduce his celebrated distinction between denotative and connotative names which at first seemed to introduce a novel variation into the theory of meaning. The variation, however, proved to be illusory, for it turned out that the connotation of a name was exhausted by a list of names which were themselves denotative, so that in the end we were left not with two kinds of names but one, viz. denotative, together with a view of different kinds of things that can be denoted by a name. Mill held, for example, that while 'the word white denotes all white things, as snow, paper, the foam of the sea etc. ... [it] connotes the attribute whiteness' (Mill, 1843, p. 19). 'Whiteness' was, of course, for him a denotative name. Consequently, given, as Mill thought, that to name something is just to mark it, whether or not a name is connotative becomes entirely dependent upon what it marks. And despite his insistence that names are the names of things and not ideas he left us in no doubt that what ultimately gets marked is something mental. The analysis of a proposition terminated in those states of consciousness by virtue of which alone we can come to know anything.

Both Bradley and Frege seized upon this, the psychological aspect of Mill's logic. When we make the judgment that snow is white, the content of the judgment was, for Mill, despite his insistence that names name things and not ideas, given in terms of those mental items in which the analysis of the names in the proposition 'Snow is white' ultimately results. Bradley saw clearly that no amount of talk about such things could serve to characterise the content of a judgment. If we are forced in the analysis of judgment to deal with ideas, and Bradley did think that we were so forced, then we need to deal with them in a way which leaves out of account their psychological status. He argued that while it might, or might not, be true that ultimately ideas are the only genuine signs, the important point was that, so far as logic is concerned, all ideas are in fact signs. Though each is 'a hard individual', and exists as a 'psychical fact', 'so long and because it keeps this character it is for logic no idea at all' (Bradley, 1883, p. 5).

This was Bradley's insight into the nature of logic, and we can see that it stemmed from his views about the content of a judgment. Expressed in his own, perhaps unfortunate, idiom it is an insight into what with regard to ideas can properly be called ideal. What he thought distinguished ideas from other mental contents is the capacity we have by means of them to form judgments, for it is only with regard to judgments that the ideality of ideas arises. His central point was that if we think of them as mental contents, if we consider them with the speciality that they have as events in our minds, we are prevented from making precisely that connection. So considered ideas would belong entirely with the reality about which judgments are made and not with the nature of the judgments that are made of it. 'The psychological idea' he insisted 'is for logic nothing but a sensible reality' (Bradley, 1883, p. 7). If our interest is in ideas as they enter into judgments their psychological characteristics are irrelevant. The big thing for logic is not to be side-tracked by such psychological irrelevancies. If, as G. E. Moore urged, Bradley himself did not always succeed in avoiding being side-tracked, the insight was, nevertheless, powerfully presented in *The Principles of Logic*.

Now if we were to have asked Bradley precisely what is wrong, from a logical point of view, in concentrating on psychological items as opposed to physical items in seeking to understand the nature of judgment, I think it is clear that he would have replied that there is nothing *particularly* wrong. We would get into the same sort of difficulties whatever items we concerned ourselves with. No amount of concentration on the physical properties of – say – marks on paper, would contribute to an understanding of what is proposed by them. The mistake Bradley was pointing to had, in the end, nothing to do with psychology at all. What it had to do with was the attempt to itemise the components of a judgment or a proposition. The central point was that if we think of a judgment as composed of things which can be named, marked or denoted, then we end up with no judgment at all, but merely with a list. 'Romeo loves Juliet' says something, whereas a list of items signified or denoted by 'Romeo', 'love', 'Juliet' does not. We can judge that Romeo loves Juliet, but we cannot judge that Romeo, love, Juliet. A list lacks the unity of a judgment or proposition, and what it lacks is what is judged or proposed. Bradley's point was that the unity of a judgment cannot be thought of as arising from the union of things that can be itemised. Though he concentrated on psychological items, his specifically anti-psychological invective did not have specifically anti-psychological roots. Rather, he saw psychologism as a prevailing orthodoxy which failed to come to grips with the nature of judgment.

Bradley saw, too, that the psychologistic temptation to think of judgment as arising from the union of ideas is particularly strong in the case of relational judgments. The judgment that Romeo loves Juliet seems to consist of two terms united by a relation. If we try to construe it as consisting of ideas then we would have to think of the relation as itself an idea. Whereas at first it looked as though the judgment contained two ideas, we now have to suppose that it contains three and we would need to invent relations to link these ideas. Yet if these relations, in their turn, are to be considered as part of the judgment, the argument just repeats itself *ad infinitum*. Relations between ideas introduced to weld ideas into a judgment cannot do the job. As part of a judgment they stand in need of welding themselves. No part of a judgment, psychologically conceived, could serve the purpose of uniting its elements. It follows that the psychological conception of judgment must be wrong. And this is what Bradley concluded. When we understand the way in which ideas enter into judgments it becomes clear that there can be no relations between them, or better, that they are not the sorts of things that can have relations between them. Russell's later criticism of this line of argument that it missed the mark because it treated relations as terms, was itself, from Bradley's point of view, an *ignoratio elenchi*, for this was the point upon which he insisted. His argument was that if a relation were part of a judgment it could only be so in the way in which anything can be part of a judgment, that is, as an idea in its ideal nature. When we understand this we are forced to the conclusion that a judgment cannot consist of linked ideas.

I have said that Bradley's idiom of 'the ideal nature of ideas' was unfortunate. I think that this is so because the term 'ideal' was inclined to make philosophers think of a form of idealism indistinguishable from the psychologism associated with Berkeley. When, for example, G. E. Moore produced his famous 'Refutation of Idealism' it was Berkeley or the writings of philosophers who used the term 'idea' in Berkeley's fashion that he had in mind. His target was the *esse est percipi* dictum. And yet that article is often thought of, and was in fact thought of by Moore himself, as confronting Bradley's views. In so far as Moore thought this he did so because he thought that Bradley had not been true to what I have described as his central logical insight. It should, nevertheless, be clear that the idealism of Berkeley was just what Bradley wished to move against.

The misreading of Bradley in the light of Berkeley nowhere shows itself more clearly than in the confused debate over the doctrine of internal relations. The treatment of it in terms of Berkelian idealistic terms is still to be found even in recent handlings of the topic. For example in *Russell and Moore: the*

Analytic Heritage we find A.J. Ayer arguing that 'Whether any property is internal to an object may be taken to depend on the way in which the object is described.' So, for example, although it is true that Scott was the author of *Waverley*, and also true that the author of *Ivanhoe* was the author of *Waverley*, neither of these two descriptions give us internal properties of Scott. And even with 'The author of *Waverley* composed *Waverley*' which looks as though it does give us an internal relation, it still remains true, Ayer urged, that 'one can attach a sense to saying that the person who was in fact the author of *Waverley* might not have been so. All that is needed for this is that he be capable of being otherwise identified' (Ayer, 1971, p. 158). So although Ayer substitutes 'description' for 'ideas' his handling of the problem is essentially the same as one which utilizes ideas thought of in Berkeley's fashion. When ideas are thought of in that way the doctrine that all relations are internal becomes absurd and, as Ryle remarked in his symposium on the topic with Moore before the Joint Session of the *Mind* and Aristotelian Society, the doctrine of internal relations becomes no longer interesting (Ryle, 1935, p. 100). It is only of interest when that way of ideas is rejected.

In any case, Bradley himself, in the Appendix to *Appearance and Reality*, had already anticipated an objection to his doctrine of internal relations along the lines presented so much later by Ayer. He was there prepared to concede, what on any account it would be hard to deny, 'that a thing may remain unaltered if you identify it with a certain character, while otherwise the thing is suffering change.'

> If, that is, you take a billiard-ball and a man in abstraction from place, they will, of course – so far as this is maintained – be indifferent to changes of place. But on the other hand neither of them, if regarded so, is a thing which actually exists ... it is a character, and that character can remain unchanged, although the existing thing is altered with its changed existence (Bradley, 1893, p. 517).

The general point which is common to both Ayer and Bradley
is that if the subject part of the judgment is what a judgment is
supposed to be about, then of course it may be internally or
externally related to what is said about it. From Bradley's point
of view, however, the subject *part* of a judgment is never what
a judgment is about, and to think so is to conceive of ideas
wrongly from the point of view of logic: it is a reversion to
psychologism. Judgments are about reality and reality itself is
not part of the judgment that is made about it. In support of
his contention he pointed to the fact that if we were to think in
such psychologistic terms we would be forced also to maintain
the absurd consequence that no judgment could be thought of
as categorical.

If a categorical judgment is one in which, as Bradley put it,
'a real assertion is made'; one in which 'some fact is asserted or
denied', then the consequence of supposing judgments to be
unions of ideas is that no judgment would be, in that sense,
categorical. We would need to think of the judgment 'S – P' as
hypothetical, i.e. as meaning that '*If* I *suppose* S, I am bound *in
that case* to assert S – P'. This, Bradley claimed, should teach us
a lesson. 'To see clearly that if judgment is the union of ideas
there can be no categorical judgment is a very great step in the
understanding of logic' (Bradley, 1883, p. 44). It is an illustration
of how pervasive the reading of Bradley's idealism in terms of
Berkeley's idealism has become, that even those who credit
Bradley, alongside Frege, with the depsychologising of logic can
continue to maintain that Bradley actually held that there are
no categorical judgments, and that all judgments in the end
are hypothetical.

Frege

If Bradley's anti-psychologism stemmed from a conception of
the nature of judgment, and therefore of the nature of logic,
Frege's did not. It is in many ways a remarkable fact of history

that the philosopher who, pretty well single-handedly, devised the means of analysing propositions, and therefore judgments, which, when thought through, requires that logic has nothing to do with psychology, does not appear himself to have derived his own anti-psychologistic impetus from that direction. When, in *The Foundations of Arithmetic*, he enumerated the three principles that he intended to keep in mind throughout the work, he commented on them in a way that makes it clear that he thought of the second (or contextual) principle, 'never to ask for the meaning of a word in isolation but only in the context of a sentence' as a corollary of the first, the depsychologising principle, 'always to separate sharply the psychological from the logical, the subjective from the objective'. The third 'never to lose sight of the distinction between concept and object' is introduced as though it were unrelated to the first two.

> In compliance with the first rule, I have used the word 'idea' always in the psychological sense, and have distinguished ideas from concepts and objects. If the second rule is not observed, one is almost forced to take as the meanings of words mental pictures or acts of the individual mind, and so to offend against the first rule as well. As to the third point, it is a mere illusion to suppose that a concept can be made an object without altering it (Frege, 1884, p. X).

The pages of the introduction which precede the enunciation of these principles contain what is generally, and rightly, considered to be the most devastating attack on psychologism in arithmetic, and it is natural to read the principles themselves as arising out of that attack. The remarkable thing is that it makes no use whatsoever of ideas about the analysis of propositions which the second and third principles clearly contain, and which are of first importance in Frege's work.

As the final clause of the first principle makes clear, Frege's anti-psychologism was, in effect, a defence of the objectivity of arithmetic. Such a defence can be produced however we break up or analyse the propositions of arithmetic. In defending the objectivity of arithmetic Frege found himself defending a Platonic third realm different from the realm of an individual's ideas and different again from the realm of material things. The trouble, from his point of view, with the Cartesian ontology is that both ideas and material things, both minds and bodies, are subject to change; there is no Archimedean point to provide the pivot for knowledge. If everything were like that, he thought, there would be no possibility of getting to know anything about the world, 'everything would be plunged into confusion'. And that is just the confusion we are in if we treat concepts as Cartesian ideas. When we treat them as such we are inclined to suppose:

> that concepts grow in the individual mind like leaves on a tree, and we think to discover their nature by studying their growth: we seek to define them psychologically, in terms of the human mind. But this account makes everything subjective, and if we follow it through to the end does away with truth. What is known as the history of concepts is really the history either of our knowledge of concepts or of the meanings of words (Frege, 1884, p. VII).

Whereas Bradley's depsychologising of judgments was ultimately a deitemising account, Frege's depsychologising of arithmetic and therefore logic remained an itemising account. His argument was that if the essential objectivity of arithmetic is to be preserved we are required to conceive of a new set of items which, like Plato's Forms, because they are timeless and unchanging, make all knowledge possible by safeguarding truth. Again, like Plato, he thought that the study of mathematics was the gateway to this timeless unchanging realm.

Frege's approach to the propositions of arithmetic was to ask what they are about. He convincingly argued that they cannot be about what our senses reveal to us since numbers are neither perceptible nor capable of being abstracted from what is perceptible. In this respect numbers are indeed like Descartes' *ideas* for these too are not perceived by us but rather had by us. On the other hand, unlike Descartes' *ideas*, and like perceptible items, they are not individuated by their unbreakable ties to the person who has them. It is in this sense that they are not subjective. When we think of numbers, while we may also supplement our thinking with visual aids such as diagrams etc. it still remains true that our thinking is not constituted either by the ideas that we have or the things that we see. Thoughts about numbers have to be distinguished from both of these. But if thoughts about numbers have so to be distinguished, it follows that thoughts themselves must be so distinguished too. Thought as such will have to be distinguished both from the perceptible and the psychological. In our attempts to get clear about arithmetic we arrive at a new area of investigation, the area of what is grasped in thought. Before we can get clear about different areas of thought like arithmetic we need first to get clear about thought itself. We need to acknowledge that thoughts are not items either of the inner or the outer world.

> A third realm must be recognised. What belongs to this corresponds with ideas, in that it cannot be perceived by the senses, but with things, in that it needs no bearer to the contents of whose consciousness to belong. Thus the thought, for example, which we express in the Pythagorean theorem is timelessly true, true independently of whether anyone takes it to be true. It needs no bearer. It is not true for the first time when it is discovered, but it is like a planet which, already before anyone has seen it has been in interaction with other planets (Frege, 1918, p. 302).

Frege's depsychologising of logic was, then, already complete prior to the development of any of his views about how a thought or proposition or judgment should be analysed. Bradley's depsychologising of logic, on the other hand, arose directly out of considerations about the nature of judgment.

This difference of emphasis between Bradley and Frege in the depsychologising of logic is crucial. Frege safeguarded the objectivity of logic by providing it with a special subject-matter, while Bradley effected his depsychologising of the subject by robbing it of a subject-matter altogether. For him, the ideal nature of ideas as they enter into judgment prevented them from becoming items of scrutiny of any kind. If Frege's way of moving from psychologism was correct, logical investigations will differ from other investigations in terms of what they are about or of what they are investigations into, while if Bradley was right in his way of depsychologising logic, then logic, and therefore philosophy, will not turn out to have a proprietory subject-matter, and we shall need to find some other way of differentiating it from other disciplines. It is noticeable that the central contentions of Part I of Russell's *Principles of Mathematics*, although influenced by Frege, as Russell himself told us, nevertheless characterise a logic depsychologised in Frege's fashion. For Russell, too, a depsychologised logic involved the delineation of a new subject-matter. The crucial Cambridge influence, however, was that of G. E. Moore.

Moore and Russell

In an article in *Mind* in 1899 entitled 'The Nature of Judgment' (an article which to the best of my knowledge has never been reprinted), Moore took Bradley to task just because he did not provide an appropriate subject-matter for logic, i.e. just because he did not provide the appropriate items which somehow make up a judgment, and that, despite his protestations to the contrary, Bradley still tied ideas as they occur in judgments too closely to *our* ideas, or ideas as they belong to an individual. Fixing upon Bradley's expression 'meaning consists of a part of the content [of an idea] cut off, fixed by the mind, and considered apart from the existence of the [idea]' Moore commented that in it Bradley had made too much of a concession to psychologism. If I am to cut off a part of my idea and consider it independently of the existence of the idea, I would first of all have to know about the idea in question, which would involve me in making some judgment about it. Moore's point was that, on Bradley's view, this judgment in its turn would involve an idea with part of its content cut off etc. and the argument would just repeat itself *ad infinitum*. Although attempting to distance his conception of judgment from ideas considered in their psychological nature, Moore claimed that in effect Bradley had not succeeded. For him the identity of the constituents of judgment were still too closely tied to mental entities. The tie between the constituents of a judgment and ideas needed to be destroyed completely. The trouble which shows itself in the infinite regress arises from trying 'to explain the concept in terms of some existent fact, whether mental or of any other nature. All such explanations do in fact presuppose the nature of the concept as a *genus per se* irreducible to anything else.' With this argument Moore had independently arrived at Frege's position; that in order to understand the nature of judgment we need a conception of a third realm, that of concepts. 'Concepts' he wrote 'are possible objects of thought; but this is no definition of them. It merely states that they may come into relation with a thinker; and in order that they *may* do anything, they must already *be* something' (Moore, 1899, p. 179).

It was *via* this article of Moore's that the movement against psychologism generated Russell's conception of logic. Moore's 'concepts' or 'possible objects of thought' became the 'terms' of Russell's *Principles of Mathematics*.

For Russell a term is defined as 'whatever may be an object of thought, or may occur in any true or false proposition, or can be counted as *one*.' Terms so conceived have, he thought, all the characteristics generally associated with substances.

> Every term, to begin with, is a logical subject: it is, for example, the subject of the proposition that itself is one. Again every term is immutable and indestructable. What a term is, it is, and no change can be conceived in it which would not destroy its identity and make it another term. (Russell, 1903, p. 44)

It was at this point in the *Principles* that Russell acknowledged in a footnote that 'the notion of a term here set forth is a modification of Mr G. E. Moore's notion of a concept' in the 1899 *Mind* article to which I have alluded.

What follows the introduction of the notion of a term in *The Principles of Mathematics* is Russell's attempt to make distinctions within the realm carved out by Moore as the subject-matter of logic; distinctions largely designed to overcome Bradley's regress. There is no doubt that he was only too keenly aware of the damage that it could do to his conception of logical theory, as the following passage makes clear.

> Consider, for example, the proposition "A differs from B." The constituents of this proposition, if we analysed it, appear to be only A, difference, B. Yet these constituents thus placed side by side do not reconstitute the proposition ... A proposition, in fact, is essentially a unity and when analysis has destroyed the unity, no enumeration of constituents will restore the proposition (Russell, 1903, p. 49–50).

However, instead of rejecting the itemising or constituent theory altogether, as I have argued Bradley did, Russell continued to insist upon it, and was therefore, as we shall see, committed to finding a technical solution. In the course of developing such a solution he found himself obliged to give some of the constituents of propositions, i.e. some terms, extraordinary properties. The trouble arose, not with those terms which are the logical counterparts of proper names, but with those which are the logical counterparts of adjectives and verbs. If Bradley's problem was to be avoided, both of these, he thought, had to be given a twofold role. While the counterparts of proper names always occur in propositions as logical subjects, the counterparts of adjectives and verbs, while retaining their character as logical subjects necessary for them to be regarded as constituents of propositions at all, needed to be thought of as having, at the same time, the capacity to perform a different function. In the case of the counterparts of adjectives they had to be thought of as capable of performing the role of denoting, and in the case of the counterparts of verbs they had to be thought of as having the capacity to give what Russell called the direction of a relation. We shall also see that both of these properties of propositional constituents ultimately generated difficulties for Russell in *The Principles of Mathematics*. We shall see that Russell thought that those about denoting were resolved by the article published five years later which Ramsey called a paradigm of philosophy, viz. 'On Denoting' which, in effect, removed the property of denoting from the logical scene.

My concern in this chapter has been to raise the question of how a depsychologised logic should be conceived. Frege and Russell, each independently, took the depsychologising of logic to entail the postulation of a special subject-matter for logic, while the import of Bradley's *Logic* was to deny logic a special subject-matter altogether. In the early part of the century the views of Russell and Frege held the field. The insight behind Bradley's depsychologising of logic was swept away along with the general demolition of Idealism. The new ideas in logic which revitalised both it and philosophy did so by making distinctions within a new subject-matter. It is with these distinctions and the problems which they raised that I shall be concerned in the following chapters.

TWO

DENOTING AND THE VARIABLE

If the subject-matter of logic is Frege's 'third realm', Moore's 'concepts' or Russell's 'terms', how can the criticism, which I have ascribed to Bradley, that no items from whatever realm, taken together, constitute a judgment or a proposition, be overcome? In the *Principles of Mathematics* this is the task Russell allocated to the capacity that some terms have to denote. His choice of the word 'denote' was, I think, unfortunate. Mill, as we have seen, had used the verb 'to denote' as a synonym for 'to name' or 'to mark', whereas Russell thought of denoting in contrast to naming. While a proper name was always for him the subject of a proposition, or what a proposition is about, even if the proposition of which it is the subject is itself part of a more complex proposition, adjectives and verbs, he insisted, play quite a different role. They occur 'in propositions in which they cannot be regarded as subject, but only as parts of the assertion', and they are 'distinguished by a capacity for *denoting*' which he made clear he intended to use in a technical sense (Russell, 1903, p. 43).

Now although Russell was not always consistent in his use of the word, and would sometimes, when he was not explicitly discussing denoting in his technical sense, fall back on something like Mill's use, it cannot be stressed too much that the task he allocated to the verb 'to denote' at the time of *The Principles of Mathematics* was a very special one. If we forget this, much of the first part of the *Principles* becomes unintelligible. Unfortunately it is all too often forgotten in modern discussions of Russell's views on denoting, which, for the most part, ignore his *Principles of Mathematics* and concentrate solely on his 1905 *Mind* article 'On Denoting'. Such discussions tend to begin by blurring a distinction that Russell took to be central, the distinction between naming and denoting. Ryle, for example, in 'The Theory of Meaning' when he was discussing Russell's views, wrote of naming or denoting as though it did not matter which you say. 'Russell', he wrote, 'found himself forced to say of some expressions which had previously been supposed to name or denote that they had to be given exceptional treatment' (Ryle, 1957, p. 362). He might equally have said 'name, denote, refer or designate' since all these words are treated by Russell commentators as though it does not matter which is used. The line of reasoning the article aroused largely centred on the general question of whether, from a logical point of view, singular terms could be eliminated. Some like Quine said yes, some like Strawson said no. Such interpretations of Russell's 'On Denoting', while clearly of intrinsic interest, are largely irrelevant to my present concern, and I suspect to Russell's own concerns as he moved from the views of the *Principles* to the views of the *Principia*.

For Russell, in *The Principles of Mathematics*, both concepts and things are, as we have seen, terms, i.e. they are logical subjects. However, while concepts as terms have the capacity to appear as logical subjects they also have the capacity to appear in propositions not as terms or logical subjects. Russell was insistent upon this, for it was his way out of Bradley's dilemma and, as we shall see, many of the difficulties in *The Principles of Mathematics*, difficulties which the 1905 article was designed, at least in part, to overcome, stem from this insistence. One and the same term, he argued, must be capable of appearing now in one way and now in another.

> It might be thought that a distinction ought to be made between a concept as such and a concept as a term, e.g. such pairs as *is* and *being*, *human* and *humanity*, *one*, in such a proposition as "this is one" and 1 in "1 is a number." But inextricable difficulties will

envelop us if we allow such a view . . . [If] there were any adjectives which could not be made into substantives without change of meaning, all propositions concerning such adjectives (since they would necessarily turn them into substantives) would be false, and so would the proposition that all such propositions are false, since this itself turns the adjectives into substantives. But this state of things is self-contradictory (Russell, 1903, p. 49–50).

This idea of a particular category of terms which have a twofold nature was meant to provide us with the means of overcoming the regress which any itemising account of the nature of propositions seems to generate. Logic has to be thought of as concerned with items, logical subjects, i.e. we remain in the third realm, but the unity of judgments, or the unity of propositions, require that some of these items have a distinctive capacity, which Russell called the capacity to denote. The very same terms, when they appear in propositions as terms, do not have this capacity. Logical subjects are named, they are not denoted. This special sense of denoting only comes into play when predicates are being considered. 'There is connected with every predicate,' Russell wrote, 'a great variety of closely allied concepts, which, in so far as they are distinct, it is important to distinguish. Starting, for example with *human*, we have man, men, all men, every man, any man, the human race, of which all except the first are twofold, a denoting concept and an object denoted' (Russell, 1903, p. 55).

Notice how in trying to express this twofold nature of concepts Russell was already in difficulties. Having insisted only a few pages earlier that the word 'term' is the word with the widest possible application, he now found himself obliged to speak of objects where the word 'object' must be taken as having a wider application than the word 'term'. He himself called attention to this in a footnote where he remarked that 'the fact that a word can be framed with a wider meaning than "term" raises grave logical difficulties' (Russell, 1903, p. 44).

Given that the idea of denoting was, as I am suggesting, introduced to deal with the anti-itemising criticism, how was it supposed do so? It would have to explain how 'Socrates is human' differs from 'Socrates, humanity'. Russell realised that we cannot explain this by saying that the first but not the second expresses a relationship between Socrates and the concept humanity, since the concept humanity would then appear as a term, i.e. as a logical subject, in the proposition which expresses the relation, and Bradley's regress would reappear. Yet they are clearly different. In the first case something is asserted of Socrates and in the second nothing is said at all. It is this that needs to be brought out but which cannot be brought out by relating terms, even terms of different kinds. Yet, on Russell's third realm or 'terms' thesis, it has to be brought out by a relating of something or other.

What, in effect, Russell did was to argue that what we have in a proposition is a relation between terms and complexes of terms which he calls objects. Concept terms denote objects when they occur in propositions other than as logical subjects, and when they do so occur the proposition asserts a relation between term and object. This relation between term and object (complex of terms), Russell thought, was not subject to Bradley's regress argument. When we say 'Socrates is human', what is said of Socrates is the same is what is said of Plato if we say 'Plato is human' and of Aristotle if we say 'Aristotle is human' etc. What, in effect, the proposition does, Russell argued, is to express a relation between Socrates and the object denoted, in his special sense of the word, by 'human'. The object is a complex of the terms 'Plato' and 'Aristotle' etc. and among the etc. is the term 'Socrates'. The term which occurs in the proposition as a logical subject is part of the complex of terms which is the object denoted by the term that does not occur as a logical subject.

Russell had fastened on to what I think is the essentially correct point that we cannot understand what it is to say something about anything unless we can also understand what it is to say the same thing about something else. It was this that he meant to capture by postulating the capacity of terms other than those which occur in propositions as logical subjects to denote in his special sense of that word. What is said is explained by means of the complex of terms of which the same thing can be said. It is as though we were to explain an unknown predicate by listing the things that it can be predicted of, with the crucial *proviso* that the idea of the list already incorporates the idea of such sayings, so that we can retain an itemising account without falling into Bradley's regress. The notion of an object differs from the notion of a term just because it is inceptive of something said. Like Russell's notion of a class it inhabits a position inter-mediate between intension and extension, the region, as he put it, where 'symbolic logic has its lair.' In fact, of course, classes, for Russell in the *Principles* were straightforwardly identified with what he there called objects. 'Our classes' he wrote, 'must in general be regarded as objects denoted by concepts, and to this extent the point of view of intension is essential. It is owing to this consideration that the theory of denoting is of such great importance' (Russell, 1903, p. 66–67). It is because of the ability of some terms to denote complexes of terms or objects that the unity of a proposition is safeguarded and Bradley's criticism fails. If terms could only appear in propositions as logical subjects Bradley's regress would be unavoidable. The fact that some terms have a dual capacity is what saves a proposition on analysis from degenerating into a list; it guarantees the unity of the proposition.

If this technical sense of 'denoting' was to save Russell's theory of terms from Bradley's regress then everything now hinged on his ability to make clear the idea of something which, while it is eternally a term, sometimes occurs in a proposition other than as a term, since it is this which does the denoting. Russell, therefore, needed some means of focusing attention on a term appearing in such a way in a proposition. It is this problem which is the central concern of chapters five, seven and eight of the *Principles*, which are entitled respectively, 'Denoting', 'Propositional Functions', 'The Variable'. Chapter six is devoted to explaining classes as the objects of denoting concepts. Russell thought that the obvious and only way to do this was by extracting from a proposition every term which appears as a term, i.e. by extracting from the proposition every logical subject that appears as a logical subject. When we have done this, he thought, what we will be left with must be what is said about those logical subjects, i.e. what we will be left with must be a term that does not occur as a term, and which in its turn will be explained by the object (or complex of terms) which it denotes.

What we have left when we extract all the terms which appear as terms in a proposition is what Russell called a propositional function. If we take the simplest case of a proposition which only has one term appearing in it as a term, e.g. 'Socrates is human', and extract that term, we are left with '. . . is human'. Russell's difficulties in making clear his technical notion of 'denoting' began precisely at this point. It soon became apparent that the gap left by the removal of the term which occurs as a logical subject needed to be indicated, otherwise we would be left with something which does not, in Russell's sense, denote, and the problem which the technical sense of denoting was introduced to solve would remain. What is left when we substract a term which occurs as a term from a proposition has to carry with it the fact that that is what it is, viz. something that is left when a term so occurring has been extracted from a proposition, because it is only this which has the capacity to denote. If there were no gap, no indication that it is a product of extraction, there would be no denoting, and what was a proposition would have become no proposition but would, once more, have been reduced to a list of logical subjects.

In the simplest case this does not seem to present us with any problems. If we symbolize the propositional function by using a letter – say – 'x' instead of the suspension points to indicate the gap sign, this might appear to be merely an elegant variation. But we have only to move to more complicated cases to see that what appears to be an elegant variation conceals a difficulty; to see, as Russell argued, that the idea of a propositional function requires the notion of the variable. The more complicated case

Russell discussed is a proposition which expresses what he called a formal implication; the proposition 'Socrates is a man implies Socrates is mortal'. When we extract from this proposition the term which on Russell's account occurs as a term what we are left with is ' ... is a man implies ... is mortal'. Russell argued that in this formula the suspension points cannot be taken to indicate mere gaps for it is essential that:

> in restoring the proposition, the *same* term should be substituted in the two places where the dots indicate the necessity of a term. It does not matter what term we choose, but it must be identical in both places. Of this requisite, however, no trace whatever appears in the would-be assertion, and no trace can appear, since all mention of the term to be inserted is necessarily omitted (Russell, 1903, p. 85).

The situation now seems to be one in which when a term is extracted from a proposition to form a propositional function, the propositional function not only has to carry with it traces that it has been formed by extraction but must carry with it indications of what has been extracted. Once more, if this is not done, propositions disintegrate on analysis, since we have no means of indicating that part of a proposition which, while it is a term, does not appear as a term, and which, therefore, has the capacity to denote. Russell's propositional functions were meant to provide us with denoting terms. Yet if we think of them merely as propositions with terms extracted they cannot do so.

It is this problem that Russell invoked the notion of the variable to solve. Propositional functions, on his account, cannot merely be thought of as propositions with a term taken out, as propositions, so to speak, with a gap in them. They must show that they are denoting expressions and this he thought they did by containing not merely a gap but a variable. The '*x*' in '*x* is human' is the sign for the variable. The job of the variable is to show that the expression of which it is a part is not a logical subject but denotes. Essentially the same point is made by Russell's invocation of the idea of constancy of form. 'When a given term occurs as a term in a proposition' he argued, 'that term may be replaced by any other while the remaining terms are unchanged. The class of propositions so obtained has what may be called a constancy of form, and this constancy of form may be taken as a primitive idea' (Russell, 1903, p. 89). It is clear that what is here meant by constancy of form is no more than the idea of the same thing being said of whatever is inserted as a logical subject, i.e. of any replaced term. Constancy of form and object denoted are essentially the same idea.

The idea of a term being replaced by any other term gives us, Russell thought, the nature of the variable.

> Taking *any* term a certain member of any class of propositions of constant form will contain that term. Thus *x*, the variable, is what is denoted by *any term*, and F*x* the propositional function is what is denoted by *the* proposition of the form F in which *x* occurs (Russell, 1903, p. 89).

Russell's idea was that since what gets denoted are objects and objects are complexes of terms, in order to explain denoting we must first of all have at our disposal some means of symbolizing *any* term. The line of thinking of the relevant chapters in the *Principles* is that in order to safeguard the unity of propositions, we need the idea of denoting. The idea of denoting requires the idea of a propositional function. And the idea of a propositional function, in its turn, requires the idea of a variable. Everything now depended upon Russell's ability to make this last notion clear. I shall address myself to the question of whether he succeeded in doing so shortly. For the present the point I am concerned to make is that once this stage in the argument has been reached, i.e. if Russell could have made the nature of the variable clear, he would have had at his disposal a means of dispensing altogether with terms that occur in propositions other than as terms: concepts as terms could have been eliminated. While there is no evidence that Russell actually realised this in the *Principles*, it was not long before he did. It was, I shall argue, the central concern of his 1905 article 'On Denoting'.

Recall first of all the argument by which Russell thought he had demonstrated in chapter IV of the *Principles* that we have need for terms that have a twofold nature. The argument was that if we tried to deny this we would be led into contradiction, since the denial would involve us in using a term in the way denied.

> [S]uppose that *one* as an adjective differed from 1 as a term. In this statement, *one* as adjective has been made into a term; hence it has either become 1, in which case the supposition is self-contradictory; or there is some other difference between *one* and 1 in addition to the fact that the first denotes a concept not a term while the second denotes a concept which is a term. But on this latter hypothesis, there must be a proposition concerning *one* as term, and we shall still have to maintain propositions concerning *one* as adjective as opposed to *one* as term; yet all such propositions must be false since a proposition about *one* as adjective makes *one* the subject, and is therefore really about *one* as term (Russell, 1903, p. 46).

Notice first of all that, besides the quickness and complexity of the argument, this passage is confusing just because it is one of those places in which Russell used the word 'denote', not in his technical sense, but in Mill's sense. The argument of the passage would not be affected if instead of 'denote' Russell had used 'refer' or 'designate'. If we do not allow ourselves to become confused by this, it will be clear that Russell was simply maintaining that we can always talk about terms occurring in propositions not as terms, (or adjectives occurring as adjectives), as I am now doing. This alone should prevent us from multiplying entities unnecessarily. On Russell's account, in the proposition 'Socrates is human' the term humanity does not appear as a term. But in what I have just said it does. It is this which forced him to conclude that there must be terms occurring in propositions that have a twofold nature; that we must not distinguish the term as it denotes from the term as logical subject, but regard them as one and the same, but with the possibility of occurring in a proposition in different ways. If, however, the role of denoting were to be entirely taken over by the variable we would have at our disposal a means of dismantling this argument. The technique for doing this was introduced in his 1905 article, where the basis of the new view was given in the following way.

> My theory is, briefly as follows. I take the notion of the *variable* as fundamental; I use $C(x)$ to mean a proposition in which x is a constituent, where x, the variable is essentially and wholly undermined. Then we can consider the two notions '$C(x)$ is always true' and '$C(x)$ is sometimes true' (Russell, 1905, p. 144).

With these tools Russell could now dispose of terms with a twofold nature. Whenever we are tempted to think of denoting as a capacity belonging to a term, i.e. as belonging to something which can be a logical subject, we can resist it, using the new technique, by saying what we want to say in such a way that no such term occurs. If, for example, we are inclined to treat what is predicted of Socrates in 'Socrates is human' as a term, i.e. turn it into a logical subject in such a proposition as – say – 'Humanity (or the property that is predicted of Socrates in "Socrates is human") is precious', we can avoid doing this by saying instead '(x) If x is human then x is precious.' By using this technique terms with a twofold nature can be made to disappear from the scene. The job they were to have done in the *Principles*, that of safeguarding the unity of the proposition, of preventing propositions on analysis from disintegrating into lists, could now be done by the variable. The problem of propositions like 'x is human implies x is mortal' was solved later, in *Principia*, by showing that we never have to consider any such proposition just like that but we have to regard it as being derived in two stages, where at each stage we only have one unrestricted variable, and that the order of stages of the derivative makes no difference. It was solved, in other words, by the axiom of the identification of real variables which is there introduced as a primitive idea. In confirmation of this way of reading Russell it might be noted that while the idea of denoting in its special sense is ubiquitous in the first part of the *Principles*, it is completely absent from the *Principia*, and that whereas quantification theory, as such, barely makes its appearance in the former, it is ubiquitous in the latter. Russell's version of quantification, in effect, solved for him the problem of the unity of a proposition. And central to his view of quantification was his theory of the variable.

The question now is, can Russell's idea of the variable be made clear? The x in 'x is mortal' was supposed to symbolize *any term*. We were supposed to get a propositional function by substituting x for a term occurring as a term in a proposition. But of course if we did this, 'x' would now have to be treated as a logical subject and the idea of denoting associated with it would not be the idea of denoting that safeguarded the unity of a proposition. The ambiguity showed up in the 1905 article where Russell first of all in the main text refers to '$C(x)$' as a proposition and then in a footnote corrected himself by saying 'more exactly a propositional function'. It is worth asking why, if the latter more exactly captured what Russell wished to say in the body of the text did he not say it there and omit the footnote? The truth of the matter was that he really wanted to have it both ways. He wanted the variable to be a logical subject so that he could use its independence from propositional functions to derive propositional functions, but he did not want it to be a logical subject otherwise what were derived would not be propositional functions but propositions. It is as though the objects of the *Principles* had not quite disappeared but had merely been replaced by a single object, a complex of terms of which all that we can say is that something can be said of them. His attempt to avoid this consequence by saying that while the variable denotes (and now this word does not have its special sense) any term it does not denote any particular term, but that it ambiguously denotes some term, or that it denotes some term without making clear which, is really only subterfuge. Frege clearly realised this when he commented upon Russell's definition of a variable as 'a symbol which is to have one of a certain set of values without its being decided which one.' His comment on this can only be described as devastating.

> Would it not be well to omit this expression ['variable'] entirely, since it is hardly possible to define it properly? Russell's definition immediately raises the question of what it means to say that 'a symbol has a value'. Is the relation of a sign to its significatum meant by this? In that case, however, we must insist that the sign be univocal, and the meaning (value) that the sign is to have must be determinate; then the variable would be a sign. But for him who does not subscribe to a formal theory a variable would not be a sign, any more than a number is. If now you write 'A variable is respresented by a symbol that is to represent one of a certain set of values' ... what is the case then? The symbol represents first the variable and, second, a value taken from a certain supply without its being determined which ... accordingly it seems better to leave the word 'symbol' out of the definition ... So we come to the definition 'A variable is one of a certain set of values, without its being decided which one'. But the last addition does not yield any closer determination, and to belong to a certain set of values, means properly to fall under a certain concept (Frege, 1912, p. 10).

Throughout the first part of the *Principles* Russell had struggled with Bradley's problem of the unity of the proposition. He there offered us a theory of terms with a twofold capacity, the capacity to appear in a proposition as a logical subject which any term by definition has, and the capacity to denote. He finally came to think that such terms could be eliminated and yet the unity of propositions safeguarded by a particular theory of the variable together with the use of quantifiers. This is the result that is presented to us in his celebrated article 'On Denoting'. The power of the so called theory of descriptions to remove problematic entities from logic and metaphysics, together with the idea of a philosophical method it generated, the method of logical fictions, I think dazzled Russell, as it dazzled his contemporaries, so much that his *Principles* worry about the unity of a proposition disappeared from sight. However, in the absence of an intelligible conception of the variable capable of performing the role which I have argued Russell allocated to it, the problem remained, even if it did not continue to occupy Russell himself. It was perhaps, although I shall not try to argue this, the ghost of the same problem that did continue to haunt him in the form of the paradoxes. Unless the variable is in some way restricted there seems to be no way of avoiding paradoxes. One way of looking at Russell's theory of Types in the *Principia* is to see it as the ghost of the denoting terms of the *Principles* which he had hoped his theory of the variable had eliminated.

THREE

CONCEPT AND OBJECT

The third of the three principles that Frege claimed to have
kept in mind while writing the *Grundlagen* was 'never to lose sight
of the distinction between concept and object.' 'It is a mere
illusion', he wrote, 'to suppose that a concept can be made into
an object without altering it.' The problem on which, as I have
argued, Russell expended so much intellectual energy in the
Principles and finally thought he had solved with his conception
of the variable and his theory of descriptions or incomplete
symbols, was ruled out from the beginning by Frege. His third
realm contains concepts and the distinction between concept
and object is absolute. Concepts can never become objects. The
idea, in Russell's language, of something which, while it is
eternally a term does not appear as a term in a proposition,
is something which Frege ruled out from the beginning. He
consequently had no use for any such notion as Russell's special
sense of denoting, since this, as we have seen, is a capacity
possessed by just such terms.

It should first of all be noticed that the fact that Frege had
no use for a notion such as Russell's special sense of denoting
should make us wary of the comparison Russell made of his
views on denoting in his 1905 article with the problems to which
Frege's distinction between sense and reference was directed.
The 1905 article is entitled 'On Denoting' and it begins by
giving examples of what Russell calls denoting phrases. The
examples which are given are the following:- a man, some man,

any man, every man, all men, the present King of France, the
centre of the mass of the solar system at the first instant of the
twentieth century, and the revolution of the sun around the
earth. All of these phrases would have been taken by Russell in
the *Principles* as introducing us to terms which have the dual
capacity discussed in the last chapter. But although these are
called denoting phrases and they are the phrases that gave
Russell the problems in the *Principles* that I have discussed in
the previous chapter, the notion of denoting had by this time
already lost the special sense which Russell had given it in the
earlier work. Now a phrase is denoting solely by virtue of its
form, by which Russell means its grammatical form, which the
examples are meant to illustrate; whereas before it was said to
denote by virtue of the role it played in a proposition. Moreover,
the theory put forward in the article has the consequence that
some of the phrases called 'denoting phrases' sometimes do not
denote at all. From this it should be clear that there is quite a
different notion of denoting at work and that the same job could
be done by the words that, as we have already seen, are often
substituted for 'denote' in discussions of Russell's views,
i.e.'designate' or 'refer'.

In the footnote in 'On Denoting' in which Russell compared
the theory he was advocating with that of Frege in 'On Sense
and Reference' he distinguished between meaning and denotation and said that in Frege's theory 'the denoting phrase
expresses a meaning' and that both the phrase and the meaning
'*denote* a denotation', whereas 'in the other theory' which he
advocated, 'there is no meaning and only sometimes denotation'.
When we try to think this through in the terms of the *Principles*
I think we are forced to the concluson that Russell took Frege's
'sinn', which he translated as 'meaning', to be the capacity of a
term to denote which he had there invoked to solve Bradley's
problem. His new theory, as I have already argued, was meant
to show that we have no need to invoke such a capacity. The
notion of 'sinn' for Frege was not, however, invoked to do that
job at all. As we have seen, he did not think that there was any

such job to do. The way in which he distinguished between concepts and objects left no room for such a job. For Frege we are only pushed into an itemising account which destroys a proposition and reduces it to a list if we wrongly treat concepts as objects, which, from his point of view, is precisely what Russell in the *Principles* had done. 'On Denoting' throws no light whatsoever on Frege's distinction between sense and reference. The references to Frege in it do, however, bring out a great deal about the change in Russell's views between 1900 and 1905.

The importance of the distinction between concept and object for Frege is obvious. The *Grundlagen* was written to defend his thesis that while numbers are indeed objects, a statement of number contains an assertion about a concept. It takes the form not only of an exposition of that view, but, negatively, of a series of demolitions of those views that take statements of numbers to be statements about objects. Such views he dismissed as 'pebble and gingerbread' arithmetic. '[A] statement of number' he argued 'contains an assertion about a concept.'

> This is perhaps clearest with the number o. If I say 'Venus has no moons', there simply does not exist any moon or agglomeration of moons for anything to be asserted of; but what happens is that a property is assigned to the *concept* 'moon of venus', namely that of including nothing under it. If I say 'The king's carriage is drawn by four horses', then I assign the number four to the concept 'horse that draws the king's carriage' (Frege, 1884, p. 59).

But now, what are we to make of 'A property is assigned to the concept *moon of Venus*'? It looks as though Frege has himself done just what he says we should never do, viz, turned a concept into an object, since 'the concept *moon of Venus*' has now become, in Russell's terms, a logical subject. Whatever the concept *moon of Venus* is it will not be a concept if we are to obey Frege's instructions and observe an absolute distinction between concepts and objects. Moreover, what can assigning a property to a concept be if there are no propositions in which such a property is assigned? If there are such propositions, then their logical subjects will be concepts, but again, that is precisely what concepts cannot be. So although Frege began by ruling out of court the problem which exercised Russell in the *Principles* it nevertheless inevitably forced itself upon him. In our discussion of judgeable contents, how can we prevent ourselves from doing what a proper understanding of judgeable contents forbids, viz. turning concepts into objects? It is to Frege's credit as a philosopher that he returned to this question time and time again. It was the main subject of his article 'Concept and Object' and it crops up over and over again in the papers that were left unpublished when he died. The importance of these writings of Frege, I shall argue, is that they show that, unlike Russell, who thought he had discovered a technical way around the problem, Frege, again to his credit, constantly acknowledged that he had not. In effect he thought that there neither was, nor could be, such a technical solution.

It is important to notice that Frege began by rejecting what Russell had finally come to think was the solution to the problem. Despite the fact that he is often credited in accounts of the development of logic with the first clear introduction of the idea of a variable, it is noticeable that every time Frege wrote about the term it was to show that it had engendered nothing but confusion. He did, indeed, lay great stress on the idea of a function, but, for him, the idea of a function was not, as it was in the end for Russell, derived by utilizing the idea of a variable. The general impression one gets on reading through Frege's writings is that he thought the term should be expunged from logic and arithmetic altogether. This is certainly the impression that is given in the passage I have already cited in the previous chapter in which he commented upon Russell's definition.

Perhaps the explanation for this is that Frege came to the idea of a function from a very different starting point from Russell. We have seen that, from the very beginning, Russell's functions were propositional functions; they were derived first and foremost by extracting a term occurring as a term from a proposition. The functions with which Frege began, however, were not propositional functions but functions as they are found in mathematics.

An expression which designates a number, such as '3^2' can be regarded as a function of the number 3. The function would then be '$(\ )^2$'. We could call this the squared function. It equally could be regarded as a function of 2 in which the case function would be '$3^{(\ )}$'. The empty brackets in each case merely indicate that the sign for a function, like functions themselves, is essentially incomplete; a space is left for the inclusion of the name of a number which completes the function and designates a value, which in this case would be another number. In order to achieve the idea of a propositional function he had to extend the idea first of all to expressions such as '$3 < 4$','$4 > 3$' and '$1 + 3 = 4$'. From each of these we can extract the name of a number. For example, in the first case we could extract the name of the number 4, leaving us with '$3 < (\ )$', which would be a functional expression which would designate a value when the name for a number is inserted in the argument place. Now, of course, the value would not be a number but, Frege says, a truth value, i.e. the true or the false. With this extension of the notion of a function the way was now open for Frege to regard the ordinary sentences such as 'Socrates is human' as designations of truth values. As such they, in their turn, could be regarded as splitting up into function and argument. Thus, for example, '$(\ )$ is human' could be regarded as a designation of the value 'the true' for the argument 'Socrates'. The way was also open for regarding concepts as special cases of functions, viz. those functions whose values are always truth values.

When we approach what Frege wrote about functions from the background of Russell's discussion of propositional functions of the *Principles of Mathematics* what is immediately striking is that they invariably begin with the observation that the nature of functions in arithmetic is obscured by a confused notion of the variable. This is true, for example of his 1904 article 'What is a function?'. Having noted that purported definitions of the word 'function' make great play with the word 'variable' he pointed out that the danger with the word is that it seems to refer us to something that varies, and that variations, of necessity, occur in time. This makes it appear that Analysis has something to do with what occurs in time. Yet it should be clear that whatever occurs in time is not relevant at all to Analysis.

> This is one of the main difficulties, one that we encounter again and again when once we try to get away from examples to the root of the matter. For as soon as we try to mention a variable, we shall hit upon something that varies in time and thus does not belong to pure Analysis. And yet it must be possible to point to a variable that does not involve something alien to arithmetic, if variables are objects of Analysis at all. (Frege, 1904, p. 107).

A few pages later he was as explicit as possible when he bluntly concluded that 'The word "variable" thus has no justification in pure Analysis.' 'If we are to provide a definition for the word "function" as it is used in Analysis' he wrote 'we must do so without availing ourselves of the word "variable".' In view of this it might seem extraordinary that histories of logic generally tell us that Frege was the first logician to introduce a clear notion of the variable. I do not wish to suggest that the histories are wrong on this point but merely to suggest that we need to be careful about just what it was that Frege did introduce a clear idea of.

From the very beginning of his *Begriffschrift* Frege distinguished between signs which have a definite meaning and signs which indicate generality. 'I divide all the symbols that I use' he wrote 'into *those that can be taken to mean various things* and *those that have a fully determinate sense*. The first kind are *letters* and their main task is the expression of generality' (Frege, 1879, p. 1). I think that an enormous amount of confusion in the reading of Frege has been caused by conflating his letters which serve to confer generality with variables as Russell described them in the *Principia*. We have seen that for Russell when a term is extracted from a proposition and a variable substituted, e.g.

when we extract 'Socrates' from 'Socrates is human' and substitute 'x', we are left with the propositional function 'x is
human'. The variable indicates that we are dealing with propositional functions. Yet this is precisely not the purpose served
by Frege's letters. The substitution of Frege's letters in the
argument place of functional expressions never yields a func-
tional expression. When Frege writes $\vdash_{\mathfrak{a}} \Phi(\mathfrak{a})$, the $\Phi(\mathfrak{a})$
does not stand for a function. The $\Phi(\mathfrak{a})$ has to be, for Frege, a
judgeable content and this it could not be if it were the sign for
a function.

Now of course there can be no radical objection to calling
Frege's letters variables, but if we do so it must be remembered
that such variables will not reveal the nature of a function.
Coming to the notion of a function from mathematics must have
made this clear to Frege. One of the difficulties which he pointed
out with regard to arithmetical notation was that the letter x is
both used to indicate the argument place of functions and as a
letter which confers generality with the resultant tendency to
generate confusion. The confusion generated is, I think, the
same confusion as we have already seen in Russell when in *On
Denoting* he first of calls '$C(x)$' a proposition and then in a
footnote a propositional function. Here is Frege's characterisation of the confusion.

> Now we sometimes speak of a function when what we have in
> mind are cases like $(1+x)^2$. Here '$1+x$' occurs in the argument
> place of the squared function. But '$1+x$' does not designate a
> function at all, but only indicates the value of a function indefin-
> itely. If in '$(1+x)^2$', we put, say, '3' in the place of 'x, then we
> get $(1+3)^2$, and here the value of the function '$1+\xi$' for the
> argument 3 is the argument of the squared function. But this
> argument is an object, a number. Here a function is compounded
> out of two functions by taking the value of the first function for
> a certain argument as an argument of the second function. In
> this connection we must persist in emphasising the fundamental
> difference of object and function (Frege, 1969, p. 239).

Now the point that I wish to stress in all of this is that Frege recognised from the beginning that we cannot allow our understanding or our explanations of generality, that is to say, we cannot allow the device of bound variables and quantifiers, to be an explanation of the way in which propositions are constituted, as I have argued Russell did after he had invented his theory of descriptions. For Frege the device of quantification required that we are able in advance to split propositions into function and argument; it could not therefore give us an explanation of this. The variable which can be bound in quantification theory will not give us the notion of a function. We need the notion of a function before we can deploy it. And if the notion of a function is meant to overcome Bradley's problem about the unity of a proposition then quantification theory will be of no help.

For Frege, then, unlike Russell, the proper expression for a function will be an expression with a gap in it. The gap or the argument place merely indicates that the name of an argument has been removed. The expression for a function will contain no proper name and no indefinitely indicating letter.

Having said all this, however, we can still ask the question what is a function and in particular what is that special case of a function which we call a concept. There seems to be no way of answering this question which does not result in a paradox. Frege himself was very well aware of this. He saw that any attempt to say what a function is necessarily fails. And since concepts are special cases of functions it follows that any attempt to give a definition of a concept necessarily fails. It is this problem which accounts for the seemingly despairing remarks in his article 'On Concept and Object' where he wrote:

> I admit there is a quite peculiar obstacle in the way of understanding with my reader. By a kind of necessity of language, my expressions, taken literally, sometimes miss my thought; I mention an object when what I intend is a concept. I fully realise that in such cases I was relying upon a reader who would be ready to

meet me halfway – who does not begrudge a pinch of salt (Frege, 1892, p. 54).

Again, at the end of the same article, he wrote:

> [O]ver the question of what it is that is called a function in Analysis, we come up against the same obstacle; and on thorough investigation it will be found that the obstacle is essential, and founded on the nature of our language; that we cannot avoid a certain inappropriateness of linguistic expression; and that there is nothing for it but to realise this and always take it into account (Frege, 1892, p. 55).

Now it is my contention that Frege was right about this; that it does indeed turn out to be the case that on thorough investigation it will be found that the obstacle is essential, and that it is indeed founded on the nature of language. However, what I take this to mean is that the problem posed by the distinction between concept and object, or, what amounts to the same thing, the problem of the unity of a proposition, what I have been calling 'Bradley's problem', is not one that has a technical solution. This is how Russell treated it and we have already seen how his solution failed. By 'technical solution' I also mean that it is not a problem for which a theoretical solution can be supplied, in any sense that we ordinarily give to the word 'theoretical'. If, therefore, Frege was right to insist that this problem is founded upon the nature of language, then it is not a problem which anything which could be called a theory of language is going to solve. In effect, if Frege was right about the problem being founded on the nature of language, we ought to be suspicious from the outset of anything which called itself a theory of language, or a theory of meaning. An idea of language which generates this problem would be an idea of language for which there could be no theory.

However, despite Frege's own insistence that the obstacle is essential, interpreters of Frege have continued to regard it as a problem which needs a technical, or theoretical, solution. Perhaps the reason for this is that philosophers in general seem to find the idea of problems to which there are not theoretical solutions hard to swallow. But in the case of the interpretation of Frege in particular there has recently emerged a more fundamental reason for ignoring his own reaction to the problem.

I am thinking of the view, held by an increasing number of philosophers since Michael Dummett first expounded it, of the position which Frege occupies in the history of philosophy. While Frege's importance in the history of logic has been recognised at least since Russell introduced him to the English speaking philosophical world, it is claimed that his philosophical importance was slow to be recognised. Dummett has persuaded many that his importance lies in effecting the decisive shift from the conception of the theory of knowledge as the basic philosophical enterprise, or as First Philosophy, as he himself puts it, a conception largely generated by the work of Descartes, to the conception of the theory of language as First Philosophy. If you think of the development of philosophy in this way then you are bound to try to find a theoretical way out of a problem which threatens the very idea of a theory of language. Here, for example is a passage from Dummett's *Frege, Philosophy of Language* which brings out why he finds what Frege says about concepts worrying.

> We can, therefore, truly say of what the expression 'the concept *horse*' stands for that it is not a concept, but an object; and, since we can speak of that for which an expression stands simply by using that expression this means that we can truly say, 'The concept *horse* is not a concept but an object.' ... [T]he paradox is intolerable because it leads to the conclusion that it is not possible, by any means whatsoever, to state, for any predicate, which particular concept it stands for, or to state for any relational or functional expression, which relation or function it stands for. Any attempt to say this must, it appears, lead to the formation of an expression which, by Frege's criteria, is a singular term, and by means of which we have not therefore succeeded in referring to a concept (or relation or function) at all but instead an object. ... Clearly, if there were no escape from this dilemma – brought to light by Frege himself – this would be a *reductio ad absurdum* of Frege's logical doctrines (Dummett, 1973, p. 212).

Dummett sees Frege's problem as one of making clear to ourselves how incomplete expressions, expressions for functions or expressions for concepts, can have a reference, and he proceeds, using one of Frege's own suggestions, to show how we can sensibly talk about what an incomplete expression stands for. His central point is that we should not take the expression 'what "x is a horse" stands for' as a singular term, and therefore should not allow it to be inserted in the argument place of a predicate expression. Just as the singular term 'Mount Everest' should be, and indeed is, substitutable for the singular term 'What "Mount Everest" stands for', so 'What "x is a horse" stands for' should be substitutable for 'x is a horse'. However, since the latter is not a singular term it follows that the former cannot be construed as a singular term either, but has itself to be construed as a predicate or an incomplete expression, i.e. it has to be construed as leaving open an argument place, i.e. as having the form 'y is what "x is a horse" stands for'. If we so construe it, he argues, then the paradox, which Frege thought essential and founded on the nature of language, can never arise, for such an expression could never be intruded into the argument place of another predicative expression. This, Dummett thinks, allows us to avoid the paradox while still maintaining the idea that incomplete expressions have a reference.

Now this would all be very well if Frege's worries were merely worries about the reference of incomplete expressions. Of course it is quite correct to point out that Frege never doubted that incomplete expressions have a reference, for that is the whole of the 'third realm' thesis. But it is not merely the having of a reference which constitutes his difficulty. The trouble is not so much that they have a reference but that we do not and cannot have any means of making a reference to what they refer to in such a way that having made such a reference we can then go on to say something true or false about what it is that we have made a reference to. In other words, the references of incomplete expressions turn out to be impervious to the theorising. The only way we have of referring to what incomplete expressions refer to is by completing the expression. But when we have done that we have not succeeded in saying anything true or false about the reference of the incomplete expression. '. . . is human' says nothing true or false because it says nothing. If we complete the expression by inserting 'Socrates' in the argument place, then, while we do say something true, i.e. that Socrates is human, nevertheless in saying that we have not said anything about what the expression '. . . is human' refers to.

Dummett's view is that if Frege's paradox is allowed to stand it constitutes the *reductio ad absurdum* of Frege's logical doctrines. My point is that it would only do this if Frege's doctrines are wrongly conceived of as providing the basis for the shift from the theory of knowledge to the theory of language. Given that this is how Dummett thinks of the importance of Frege in the history of philosophy it is easy to understand the attitude he takes to Frege's problem. If we are convinced that the decisive turning point in recent history was the move from the theory of knowledge to the theory of meaning or the theory of language, then Frege's paradox does present us with a theoretical impasse. If a theory of language requires us to split sayables into absolutely different items such that when they are brought together what is said is reconstituted, then, from a theoretical point of view, we are in a hopeless situation if the theory dictates that we cannot say anything about half of the items into which sayables are split. From the moment of its birth the theory of language as First Philosophy would turn out to be no philosophy at all. The problem over concepts would only be a *reductio ad absurdum* of Frege's logical doctrines if the importance of those doctrines were their contribution to the theory of language. We have seen, however, that Frege himself came to the view that if the unity of a proposition or judgeable content is to be preserved the idea of a *theory* of language results in paradox. The upshot of Frege's writing about language was, I think the destruction of the idea that language from a logicial point of view is something that we can theorise about, in the most generally accepted sense of what theorising is. That is to say, language, from a logical point of view, is not something about which it makes sense to seek to produce an organised body of truths. Any attempt to produce a single truth, let alone an organised body of truths, will always fail to capture what is essential to language, viz. that in language things can be said. A logical interest in English or German sentences has nothing to do with the fact that they are English or German sentences but in what is said by means of them. The upshot of Frege's pioneering work was the conclusion that when what is said, or better the capacity to say things, is the subject of our interest in language, our theorising efforts invariably let us down. I shall argue in the next chapter that Wittgenstein was led to the same conclusion in the *Tractatus*.

FOUR

COLOURLESS OBJECTS

When we approach Wittgenstein's *Tractatus Logico Philosophicus* from the background of problems about the unity of a proposition, that is from the background of the problem which for Russell in *The Principles of Mathematics* required a special sense of 'denoting', and for Frege required a radical distinction between concept and object, it looks a very different work from the way in which it has often been presented. One way to bring this out is to consider the status of 'objects' in the work.

The *Tractatus* tells us that the analysis of propositions ultimately results in elementary propositions which are concatenations of names. These names name objects which are simple. Now many commentators find themselves puzzled that Wittgenstein did not provide us with any examples either of elementary propositions or of objects. For example, David Pears, in a book on Wittgenstein published in 1971 wrote:

> It is mystifying to introduce elementary propositions without explaining what they are. But there is a real difficulty here. Wittgenstein did not claim to be able to give any examples of elementary propositions, because he thought that neither he nor any other philosopher had yet got down to the ultimate components of factual propositions (Pears, 1971, p. 59).

Two years later, Anthony Kenny in his book on Wittgenstein wrote in much the same vein:

We are given no information in the *Tractatus* as to what kinds of things simple objects are ... It is not even clear whether the simples would be particular individuals or universal types ... But this lack of clarity accords with Wittgenstein's insistence that it is only *a priori* that he knows of the existence of simples, not that he can give any examples (Kenny, 1973, p. 85)

In a later article he attempted to sustain the thesis that Wittgenstein in his later work was careless as a critic, misrepresenting not only the work of Frege and Augustine but also his own early work. He tried to show that 'he came to misrepresent the *Tractatus* on the nature of names, on the nature of objects, on the nature of facts, and on the nature of propositions' (Kenny, 1974, p. 4). Waiving the point that if Wittgenstein did, through carelessness, or for whatever reason, manage to misrepresent the *Tractatus* with regard to all of these there would be little left of the *Tractatus* for him to get right, and concentrating entirely on the nature of objects, we find that the evidence that Kenny adduced for his 'careless critic' thesis was that while the *Tractatus* is written in such a way as to be neutral with regard to whether objects are individuals or universals, and that this neutrality is preserved throughout the conversations with Waismann, nevertheless, in various places in his later work Wittgenstein did use as examples to illustrate objects, colours considered as universals and also sometimes spoke of them as though they were Platonic Ideas.

Responding to this criticism of carelessness P. M. S. Hacker took the view that what may look like carelessness when construed as a representation of his own earlier views becomes accuracy when regarded as criticism. He claimed that 'the concept of an object in the *Tractatus* is *incoherent*, and there are or could be no such entities.' On such an account it would not matter what you took as an example of an object; it would always be possible to show the incoherencies in it. 'Only in a Pickwickian sense' he argued 'can one coherently misrepresent what is logically incoherent. What one can do is to represent the sources of the incoherence, and this is precisely what Witt-genstein does.' (Hacker, 1975, p.111). Both the view that Witt-genstein was careless as an expositer of his own early conception of objects and the view that he was an accurate critic of it assume that on that conception it would have at least to make sense to give examples of objects even if no-one is yet in a position to do so. On either view objects are thought of as items or entities.

This puzzlement about 'objects' in the *Tractatus* is related to the picture that is generally presented of Wittgenstein as some-one who, through his conversations with Russell, produced in the *Tractatus* a version of Russell's logical atomism, just as Russell himself acknowledged that the lectures he gave under the title of 'Logical Atomism' were greatly influenced by the con-versations he had had with Wittgenstein. Kenny's book actually charts the development of Wittgenstein's thought in chapters entitled 'The Metaphysics of Logical Atomism' and 'The Dis-mantling of Logical Atomism', even though he is well aware that the only atomic things referred to in the *Tractatus* are atomic propositions. However, for our purposes it is important to notice that Russell's lectures were given at a time when, as I have argued, the problem of the unity of the proposition no longer worried him. He thought it had been overcome by his notion of the variable, the theory of quantification which it permitted, and his idea of an incomplete symbol. These taken together provided him with the theory of logical fictions; a new philo-sophical tool which could be used to analyse away putative entities; a new Ockham's Razor which only genuinely logical atoms could resist. Such things, for Russell at this period, turned out to be the items of direct perception, items of which we have knowledge of acquaintance and not knowledge by description, in effect Moore's sense data or Hume's impressions, but certainly not the 'concepts' of Moore's 'Nature of Judgment' article. Yet Wittgenstein's 'objects' are, as we shall see, the heirs to Moore's 'concepts'. The ascription to Wittgenstein of a philosophy of logical atomism, in anything like Russell's sense, is I think, just a mistake; even if it is a mistake which sometimes looks as though it is sanctioned by some of the remarks which Wittgenstein himself made in the early sections of the *Philosophical Investigations*.

The first thing that should be noticed about Wittgenstein's 'objects' is that, unlike Russell's items of acquaintance, but like the 'terms which denote' of the *Principles*, they are inceptive of the propositions in which they can occur. However since propositions in the *Tractatus* are thoughts made perceptible to the senses, the correct way to say this, in the *Tractatus*'s own vocabulary, is to say that objects are inceptive of the thoughts in which they can feature. If the existence of a state of affairs is a fact, and a thought is a logical picture of a fact, then, given that 'It is essential to things that they should be possible constituents of states of affairs' (2.011), together with its corollary that 'If I know an object I also know all its possible occurrences in states of affairs. (Every one of these possibilities must be part of the nature of the object)', (2.0123), we must conclude that it belongs to the nature of an object that it can feature in a state of affairs and therefore a thought. But even this is to weaken Wittgenstein's conception of objects, for outside of the way in which they enter into states of affairs there is nothing to be said of objects at all. It is difficult to see how his remark that 'In a manner of speaking objects are colourless' can be read in any other way.

The remark occurs as the culmination of a series of remarks in which the notions of 'objects' 'possible occurrences in states of affairs', 'substance' and 'form' are interwoven. Since the line of thinking which leads up to this remark is central to my purpose I shall quote it in full.

2.021   Objects make up the substance of the world. That is why they cannot be composite.

2.0211   If the world has no substance, then whether a proposition had sense would depend upon whether another proposition was true.

2.0212   In that case we could not sketch out any picture of the world (true or false).

2.022 It is obvious that an imagined world, however different it may be from the real one, must have *something* – a form – in common with it.

2.023 Objects are just what constitute this unalterable form.

2.0231 The substance of the world *can* only determine a form, and not any material properties. For it is only by means of propositions that material properties are represented – only by the configuration of objects that they are produced.

2.0232 In a manner of speaking, objects are colourless.

These remarks, as the numbering system indicates, are comments on 2.02 'Objects are simple'.

All of the difficulties that commentators have experienced with these passages stem from a refusal, or an unwillingness, or an inability, to do what it should be clear Wittgenstein was urging us to do in them, viz. to identify, or to treat as the same, objects, substance and *form*. When we try to read these passages with something like a Fregean sense of 'object' in mind they appear to be, as J. O. Urmson described them, a set of 'somewhat Heracleitian utterances' or a series of 'obscure apophthegms' made all the more obscure by the complete absence of any examples. Urmson's comments show that he was trying to think through the remarks with Frege's sense of object, or, perhaps, what might be called an ordinary sense of object in mind; the sense in which you could point to an object or pick up one. His gloss, for example, on 2.0231 makes this clear. He read it as saying that 'What objects there are determines what can be the case, but not what actually is the case. If a red patch were an object, then its existence would determine what is the case – that something was red' (Urmson, 1956, p. 59).

'If a red patch were an object', in other words if only we could indicate an object, find an example of one, the passages would be less obscure. As for 2.0232, he thought that 'This is a way of saying that objects are what can be red, &c., not what is already of one of these colours' (Urmson, 1956, p. 59). If Wittgenstein's own remarks seem obscure such comments only serve to deepen the obscurity, for it is entirely baffling how saying that objects are 'in a manner of speaking colourless' can be a way of saying that they can be red.

I have used Urmson as an illustration because his way of reading the passages brings out in the clearest way I know the absurdities that ensue if we take Wittgenstein's objects to be items that stand in need of identification. Once we are clear about this it should also be clear how any attempt to give examples of objects is not just impractical, or difficult, or must wait upon further analysis, but nonsensical. If we were able to give examples then that very fact alone would show that what we were exemplifying would not be an object. Whereas Russell's 'logical atoms' cry out for identification, since they are the items that remain when the method of logical fictions has been exhausted, Wittgenstein's objects resist identification, not because they are difficult items to identify, but because they are not items to be identified. With Wittgenstein's 'objects' we have returned to Bradley's rejection of the itemising account altogether. The difference is that whereas in Bradley this led to a form of idealism which resulted in a disparagement of, or scepticism about, logic, for Wittgenstein the result is exactly the opposite. The nature and importance of logic and logical investigations only becomes apparent once the itemising approach is seen to be bankrupt.

The *Tractatus*, Wittgenstein wrote in his preface, 'deals with the problems of philosophy and shows ... that the reason why these problems are posed is that the logic of our language is misunderstood.' Unfortunately, Wittgenstein's own talk about 'the logic of our language' has itself proved easy to misunderstand. When it is approached from the background of Russell's 'Lectures on Logical Atomism' it is bound to be misunderstood. The definite article creates the impression that there is something that can be called the logic of our language which a correct analysis of the sentences of our language will unearth; something which while contained in language is nevertheless hidden by the language which contains it; something which it is the business of philosophical analysis to reveal. After the

publication of the *Tractatus*, the joint impact of it and Russell's
lectures was to make the idea that our ordinary language conceals logical form into something of a rallying cry. It seemed to
provide philosophy with a programme; one of devising ways of
exhibiting 'the logic of our language' and of showing how bad
philosophy is a result of misunderstanding it. Urmson's book is in
fact a good characterisation of the way in which this programme
developed. I shall later try to show how in recent times, largely
inspired by the work of Donald Davidson, there has been a
return to this philosophical programme, with Tarski's theory of
truth doing duty for a theory of meaning, and so allowing this
conception of logical form to be brought once more into the
centre of the picture. Wittgenstein's contribution to this development continues to be seen through the eyes of Russell's introduction to the *Tractatus*.

For the Russell of the 'Lectures on Logical Atomism' (unlike
the Russell of the *Principles*) we have arrived at the logical form
of a proposition when we have isolated the simples which it
contains and know the relations in which they stand, and this
is just the view which he attributes to Wittgenstein in his introduction.

> A fact that has no parts that are facts is called by Mr Wittgenstein
> a *Sachverhalt*. This is the same thing that he calls an atomic fact.
> An atomic fact, although it contains no parts that are facts
> nevertheless does contain parts. If we may regard 'Socrates is
> wise' as an atomic fact we perceive that it contains the constituents
> 'Socrates' and 'wise'. If an atomic fact is analysed as fully as
> possible ... the constituents finally reached may be called 'simples'
> or 'objects' ... [P]ropositions presuppose the naming of simples.
> In this way the naming of simples is shown to be what is logically
> first in logic (Wittgenstein, 1921, p. xiii).

Now it should be clear that this idea of naming simples having
priority in logic, and the idea of form that goes with it, cuts
quite against the grain of the *Tractatus*. It is for this reason that
many philosophers have found themselves baffled when they
have tried to read Wittgenstein's discussion of simples in the

early sections of the *Philosophical Investigations* as a direct attack on his conception of simple objects in the *Tractatus*.

Although I do not, of course, suggest that Wittgenstein wrote with Moore in mind, nevertheless his conception of 'objects' reveals itself to be the heir to Moore's concepts in that it gives his working through of the problem to which Moore's 'concepts' were meant to be a solution. The realm of Moore's concepts is a realm in which the problem Bradley had noticed with the psychologising account of the constituents of propositions is meant to be overcome. The opening sections of the *Tractatus* should have made it clear that in Wittgenstein's view this problem is only overcome when we cease to think of propositions as having, in any ordinary sense of the word, constituents at all. A corollary of this is that if getting at the constituents of propositions is meant to be revelatory of logical form we need a radically different conception of logical form from that provided by Russell. Even if, as Wittgenstein acknowledged, it was Russell 'who performed the service of showing that the apparent logical form of a proposition need not be its real one', nevertheless, finding the logical form of a proposition could not for him consist in identifying its components and discovering the relations in which they stand to each other. It follows that the ways in which we speak about the make-up of a proposition, i.e. about form, will need to be radically different from the ways in which we speak about anything else. In particular it will not amount to saying what the components of a proposition are and how they are related to each other. The concepts which capture the make-up of propositions, i.e. the concepts which capture logical form, formal concepts, will have to be distinguished from concepts proper. At 4.127 Wittgenstein tells us how the distinction is to be made.

4.127   The propositional variable signifies the formal concept, and its values signify the objects that fall under the concept.
4.1271   Every variable is the sign for a formal concept. For every variable represents a constant form that all its values possess, and this can be regarded as a formal property of those values.

4.1271   Thus the variable name 'x' is the proper sign for the pseudo-concept *object*. Wherever the word 'object' ('thing', etc.) is correctly used, it is expressed in conceptual notation by a variable name. For example, in the proposition, 'There are 2 objects which . . . ', it is expressed by '$(x,y) . . .$'. Wherever it is used in a different way, that is as a proper concept-word, nonsensical pseudo propositions are the result. So one cannot say, for example, 'There are objects', as one might say, 'There are books'.

Now, while these passages show clearly that it is wrong from Wittgenstein's point of view to ask for examples of objects, the relationship between the idea of a variable, and the idea of form that is here being made use of, is not exactly pellucid; at least not given the difficulties that we have seen are engendered by Russell's account of the variable. If every variable is the sign for a formal concept then in order to sustain the thesis that what we find in the *Tractatus* is a very different conception of logical form from that attributed to him by Russell in his introduction, we need to bring out how this is reflected in the use Wittgenstein makes of the notion of a variable in the *Tractatus*. In particular we shall need to show how it differs from Russell's.

We have seen how after 1905 Russell maintained that from a logical point of view the unrestricted variable is all that is needed and that the hallmark of the unrestricted variable is its ambiguity. It features in a propositional function as a logical subject, but one which is wholly undetermined. 'When we speak of "Fx" where "x" is not specified we mean one value of the function but not a definite one.' The 'x' in 'Fx', just because it is an unspecified argument place filler is at least an argument place filler, and as such is distinguished from the function whose argument place it fills. We are required to be able to think of *any term* independently of the propositions in which it can occur, and it is this which enables us to generate propositional functions and ultimately the theory of quantification. Russell's conception of logical form goes with this conception of the variable. It was therefore perfectly sensible, from his point of view, to seek to identify the ultimate argument place fillers, those items which remain when the method of logical fictions is exhausted and which are ambiguously denoted by the variable, i.e. are ambiguously denoted by *any term*. David Pears has shown how this programme was extended even further by Russell in a work entitled *Theory of Knowledge* left unpublished, it is alleged, because of the criticisms that Wittgenstein made of it (Pears, 1977, p. 177). In that work Russell had argued that not only must we be acquainted with the terms a,R,b of a relational proposition 'aRb' but also that we must be acquainted with the general form of such a proposition given by the symbol '$x \xi y$' in which all the terms had been replaced by variables. In other words not only must we be acquainted with the terms which go to make up the proposition but we must be acquainted with the general form 'something is related to something'.

It should now be clear, however, that although Russell attributes his original conception (i.e. minus the extension to a general form) to Wittgenstein in his introduction to the *Tractatus* it is not at all the conception that is being deployed in that work. Wittgenstein adopted a quite different conception of the variable and therefore a quite different conception of logical form from that deployed by Russell. His 'The general propositional form is a variable' (4.53) cannot be given a Russellian reading.

First of all notice that the connection between the variable and a thought made visible to the senses, i.e. a proposition, is intimate. Without propositions there are no variables. There is no suggestion in the *Tractatus* of the possibility of indicating *any term* independently of its occurrence in a proposition. 'All variables can be construed as propositional variables. (Even variable names)' (3.314). Although Wittgenstein tells us that like Russell and Frege he regards a proposition as a function of the expressions it contains, it remains an open question as to how this is to be understood. An expression (or symbol) in the *Tractatus* is any part of a proposition which characterises its sense. (3.31) As such, we are told, it presupposes the forms of all the propositions in which it can occur (3.311), so that it is 'presented by means of the general form of the propositions that

it characterises' (3.312). The form of the propositions in which
an expression can occur is what Wittgenstein calls a variable.
An expression or a symbol, i.e. any part of a proposition, is
properly thought of as a variable proposition. 'If we turn a
constituent of a proposition into a variable, there is a class of
propositions all of which are values of the resulting variable
proposition' (3.315). A part of a proposition is therefore, for
Wittgenstein, a propositional form. Just as objects cannot first
of all be identified and then discovered to stand in certain
relations to each other, so parts of propositions cannot first of
all be identified and then fitted into propositions. One of the
reasons why I have resisted the temptation to translate 'satz' as
'sentence' is that if we translate it in that way this point becomes
wellnigh incomprehensible. Sentences do have parts which can
be independently identified and then juxtaposed. I shall argue
later that one of the motives behind the linguistic turn in philosophy associated largely with Oxford after 1945 was the belief
that while thoughts do not have parts, the sentences which
express them do, so that we can get at the parts of thoughts by
considering the parts of sentences in which they are expressed.
The reason why I think it is wrong to translate 'satz' by 'sentence' is that it would be difficult by means of that word to make
Wittgenstein's point. If a proposition is a thought made visible
to the senses then the sense in which it can be said to have parts
has to be the sense in which a thought has parts. That is why a
part of a proposition can only be presented by means of a
propositional variable or a variable proposition.

When Wittgenstein says that like Frege and Russell he regards
a proposition as a function of the expressions which it contains,
we cannot read this as saying that there are expressions which
the proposition contains, namely so and so and such and such,
and the proposition is a function of them, since expressions are
already variable propositions. In the sense in which Frege might
say that 3^2 is a function of 3 we cannot say that a proposition is
a function of one of its expressions or parts, since outside of the
propositions there could be no way of saying what those parts

are. With Wittgenstein's notion of an expression or symbol we are still in the realm of Russell's problems in the *Principles*, where a propositional function had to carry with it the idea of the propositions in which it could feature. We have seen how Russell solved this problem by his theory of the variable, and the idea of denoting terms as incomplete symbols, which in turn allowed him to develop the notion of logical form which he attributes to Wittgenstein in the introduction to the *Tractatus*. Wittgenstein's insistence that expressions are variables and all variables are propositional variables or variable propositions cuts off the route to any such conception of form.

This idea that a part of a proposition is a propositional variable or a variable proposition; that the general form of a proposition is a variable; with its corresponding effect on the way in which we think of logical form, helps us with what Wittgenstein called the vexed question of internal and external relations, for internal relations are relations between forms. How we conceive of them depends upon how we conceive of logical form, i.e. on how we conceive of objects. This brings us to what Wittgenstein himself called the fundamental insight in the work; the distinction between what can be said and what can be shown.

We have already seen in chapter one how Bradley's view about internal relations was wrongly handled because of a mistaken account of his views on the constituents of judgment. If we think of judgment as having identifiable parts, let us say, a subject part and a predicate part, then it makes sense to ask whether the subject part could remain the same while the predicate part was changed. Sometimes the answer will be 'Yes' and sometimes the answer will be 'No'. It all depends, as Ayer put it, on the way in which the subject is described or identified. This seemed to make nonsense of Bradley's contention that all relations are internal, that a change in a relation implies a change in a term. This criticism of Bradley's doctrine of internal relations in terms of a doctrine about judgment which requires that they have independently specifiable parts, what I have been calling an itemising account of judgments, is one which we have already seen Bradley rejected. If, therefore, a similar account of propositions is also rejected in the *Tractatus* we should also expect to find there a quite different account of the difference between internal and external relations than the one I have used Ayer to illustrate. And this is what we do in fact find.

> 4.121   The existence of an internal property of a possible situation is not expressed by means of a proposition: rather it expresses itself in the proposition representing the situation, by means of an internal property of that proposition.
>
> It would be just as nonsensical to assert that a proposition had a formal property as to deny it.

Now how are we to understand this phrase 'it expresses itself in the proposition representing the situation'? Suppose we take the proposition 'Socrates is wise'. Russell, as we have seen, would take this, at least for the sake of illustrating his views of logical form, as being made up of the items 'Socrates' and 'wise'. If the proposition is true then these two items are related to each other in a particular way. To ask whether the relation is an internal or an external one is to ask whether 'Socrates' would remain 'Socrates' if he were not related in that way to 'wise'. If the answer is 'Yes' then the relation is an external one. If the answer is 'No' then the relation is an internal one. In other words, the conception of form that Russell had developed dictated what he said about the distinction between internal and external relations. It should be obvious by now that such an answer was not open to Wittgenstein. If the constituents of propositions are not identifiable independently of the propositions of which they are components, then the questions which Russell needed to ask to become clear about the difference between internal and external relations cannot be asked, since there is nothing for them to be asked about. Moreover, we can see that Wittgenstein was right on this issue just by asking ourselves what is the relation which 'Socrates' holds to 'wise' if the proposition 'Socrates is wise' is true? If we try to say 'Socrates possesses the property wisdom' then either that just means the same as 'Socrates is wise' in which case we are no further forward, or it means something different, in which case we are presented with the problem of how the possession of one property, that of having the property wisdom, explains the having of a quite different property, that of being wise. Moreover, if we were to ask about the constituents of the proposition 'Socrates has the property wisdom' Russell would have to say that they were 'Socrates' and 'the property wisdom' which stand in a certain relation to each other if that proposition is true. But we had better not ask what that relation is lest another property for 'Socrates' to be related to appears on the scene. It was no doubt this which prompted him in his discarded *Theory of Knowledge* to introduce acquaintance with general propositional forms which, while necessary for the understanding of propositions must not be thought of as constituents of the propositions they enable us to understand.

The conception of objects which Wittgenstein characterises by saying that 'objects are in a manner of speaking colourless' has, then, its counterpart in the idea that a part of a proposition which contributes to its sense, i.e. an expression or a symbol, is a variable proposition. It is this which makes his conception of logical form quite different from Russell's, and which also engenders a quite different conception of internal relations, since internal relations are relations between forms.

With Wittgenstein's notion of a variable proposition or propositional form comes his idea of internal relations between propositions. A part of a proposition, i.e. an expression or symbol, gives us what is common to a group of propositions. But we run into insuperable difficulties if we try to say what it is they have in common. We cannot just bluntly say that they contain the same symbol, expression or part, since on the account that Wittgenstein gives of the nature of a symbol, in order to understand 'same symbol' we would need to refer to the propositions in question. In order to understand what it is for propositions to be what they are, i.e. thoughts made visible to the senses, we need to understand what it is for propositions to have something in common in such a way that the question 'What is it that they have in common?' is not a question that can sensibly be asked, if asking it presupposes that an answer would state the common factor. The notion of a part of a proposition that can serve to characterise its sense involves the idea of unsymbolisable, unexpressable relations between propositions. A propositional variable is the prototype of a proposition. What is common to the propositions which are the values of the variable is a certain form or structure; which is what we mean when we say that such propositions exhibit internal relations.

How, then, do internal relations differ from relations proper? Consider the relational proposition 'London lies to the south of Newcastle'. In order to get at the contribution to the sense of the proposition made by its parts we shall need to hold one part of it constant while allowing the rest of it to vary. So initially we might have 'London lies to the south of ... '. The same operation can be performed again giving us '... lies to the south of ... '. We now have a propositional variable or variable proposition which has for its values all of those propositions in which suitable candidates can be substituted in the argument places. The contribution which the variable proposition ' ... lies to the south of ... ' makes to the proposition 'London lies to the south of Newcastle' is an internal or structural relation between those propositions. It is by virtue of such relations that relational propositions make sense.

When we think of internal relations in this way we can begin to understand the otherwise baffling remark in the notes which Wittgenstein dictated to Moore.

> Internal relations are relations between types which cannot be expressed in propositions, but are all shown in the symbols themselves, and can be exhibited systematically in tautologies. Why we come to call them 'relations' is because logical propositions have an analogous relation to them to that which properly relational propositions have to relations (Wittgenstein, 1969a, p. 115–116).

At first sight this is baffling for we would be inclined to say that relational propositions express relations. Yet we know that

Wittgenstein would not allow that logical propositions express relations between types. Such relations, he thought, could not be expressed in propositions at all. However, given that the sense contributed to a relational proposition by the symbol for a relation is the internal relation between those propositions which contain it, it becomes obvious that such a contribution is not something which could itself be expressed in a proposition. This is why it can be said to stand to relations proper as logical propositions stand to relations between types.

The depsychologising of logic initiated a search for the proprietory subject matter of logic; Frege's 'third realm', Moore's 'concepts', and Russell's 'terms'. While Wittgenstein's objects at first appeared to be, and still continue to be thought of as, the most refined candidates for the job, what they in effect showed was that the job does not exist. Logic, on this account, turns out not to have any subject matter about which an organised body of truths can be produced. This is how we should read his remark 'Logic must take care of itself.' Logical form, for Wittgenstein shows itself in the things we say. It is not itself something about which there is a need for something to be said. That is why 'What we cannot speak about we must pass over in silence.'

FIVE

CATEGORIES OF LINGUISTIC EXPRESSION

In the 'fifties and 'sixties it was common to think of Gilbert Ryle's work in conjunction with that of the later Wittgenstein. His book *The Concept of Mind*, published in 1949, was so influential that for almost three decades any writing on the philosophy of mind had to begin by a consideration of it. While there is some evidence that his attention was first of all focused upon the problem of the freedom of the will, the residue of which is the chapter on the will in *The Concept of the Mind*, what he in the end produced was a devastating attack on Descartes' conception of the mind. This came to be read in conjunction with Wittgenstein's *Blue and Brown Books* which although not published until much later had enjoyed a large circulation in typescript, and also in conjunction with the *Philosophical Investigations* posthumously published in 1953. Ryle's attack on the Cartesian conception of the mind was generally thought to be entirely harmonious with the anti-private language sections of the *Philosophical Investigations*. More importantly for our present purposes, however, Ryle himself described the book as a 'philosophical book written with a meta-philosophical purpose'. The meta-philosophical purpose was to illustrate the efficacy of a new conception of logic and logical investigations in solving or resolving large scale philosophical problems. The new conception of logic and logical investigations was thus associated with Wittgenstein's later work and in consequence Ryle's work, although quite different in style from Wittgenstein's, was looked upon as a version of

Wittgenstein's later views. I shall argue that this idea of hom-
ogeneity of view but heterogeneity of style was an illusion. The
major influence of Wittgenstein on Ryle's thinking was the
Tractatus, and his development of what he took to be the *Tractatus*
position, particularly with regard to the problem of propositional constituents, which is my central concern, was very
different from Wittgenstein's own.

The turning point in Ryle's philosophical development was
when, as he himself put it in the autobiographical introduction
he wrote for a collection of essays on his work, he went 'all
Cambridge'. The Cambridge that impressed him was the Cambridge of Russell. 'My interest' he wrote 'was in the theory of
meaning.'

> I laboured on the doublets: Sense and Reference, Intension and
> Extension, Concept and Object, Propositions and Constituents,
> Objectives and Object, Facts and Things, Formal Concepts and
> Real Concepts, Proper Names and Descriptions, Subjects and
> Predicates. It was in Russell's *Principles of Mathematics*, in his
> Meinong articles and his 'On Denoting' that I found the pack-
> ice of logical theory cracking (Ryle, 1970, p. 7).

We can see that Ryle's 'doublets' all belong to the problematic
area with which I am concerned. It is clear also that Ryle saw
his own work as a development of some of Russell's ideas.
Two of these ideas we have already discussed; the idea of an
incomplete symbol and the related notions of propositional function and the variable. Although he made no use of these terms
in his own writings, he did make it clear that the problems which
engaged him were those for which Russell invented these terms.
Two rare Rylean footnotes in Volume 2 of the *Collected Papers*
bring out this point. The first occurs at the end of 'Systematically
Misleading Expressions' published in 1932 where Ryle wrote:

> In this paper I have deliberately refrained from describing
> expressions as 'incomplete symbols' or quasi things as 'logical
> constructions'. Partly I have abstained because I am fairly ignor-
> ant of the doctrines in which these are technical terms, though in
> so far as I do understand them, I think I could restate them in

words which I like better without modifying the doctrines. But partly, also, I think that the terms themselves are rather ill-chosen and are apt to cause unnecessary perplexities. But I do think that I have been talking about what is talked about by those who use these terms, when they use them (Ryle, 1932, p. 62–62).

The second comes from his article 'Categories' published in 1938.

I apologise, not very humbly, for the terminology which, here and elsewhere in this paper, I substitute for the terminology of 'propositional functions', 'variables', 'values' and the rest. I do so for the simple reason that this terminology has led to many confusions. Especially it failed to make obvious whether in talking of functions, variables, values, etc. we are talking of certain expression or talking *with* certain expressions *of* certain sorts of things. Should we say that Socrates or 'Socrates' is the value of the variable in 'x is snub-nosed'? The terminology which I use is meant to be overtly semantic. Its items too are meant to be reasonably self-explanatory (Ryle, 1938, p. 176).

We can see from both of these footnotes the movement into the semantic or linguistic idiom which was characteristic of Ryle and became characteristic of a generation of philosophers; the movement which, as I shall argue, constituted his solution to the problem of the nature of propositional constituents which he inherited from Russell, Frege and Wittgenstein.

The idea that impressed him was the idea that we have seen so much depressed Frege. When we are philosophising we seem to be constrained to speak about concepts. Philosophers are interested in the substantive contributions which concepts make to propositions. It is one thing to understand that if Socrates is wise then either Plato is mortal or Socrates is wise, it is quite another thing to understand what it means to say of Socrates that he is wise. For that, it seems, we need to know about the concept of wisdom. If concepts were themselves detachable parts of propositions they could then be made the subjects of further propositions. However, Ryle had learned from Frege and Wittgenstein that this is just what cannot be done. 'The philosopher' he wrote 'has apparently to try not just to deploy but to describe the concepts with which he is concerned.'

> He has to try to say what Pleasure and Existence are. He has to try, necessarily in vain, to attach object-characterising predicates to non-object-mentioning expressions. But by no prestidigitation can the live verb 'enjoys' or the live verb 'exists' (except in inverted commas), be made grammatical subjects to live verbs. The philosopher's description of a concept is bound to terminate in a stammer (Ryle, 1962, p. 187).

He even thought he had detected a model for displaying this point in Plato's talk about letters and syllables towards the end of the *Theaetetus*, provided that the model was construed phonetically. In a paper entitled 'Letters and Syllables in Plato' he argued that the:

> phonetic model of letters and syllables would be an almost perfect model by means of which to express Frege's difficult but crucial point that the unitary something that is *said* in a sentence or the unitary sense that it expresses is not an assemblage of detachable sense atoms, that is, of parts enjoying separate existence and separate thinkability, and yet that one truth or falsehood may have discernible, countable and classifiable similarities to and dissimilarities from other truths and falsehoods. Word meanings or concepts are not proposition components but propositional differences (Ryle, 1960, p. 58).

If it is the case that concepts are not propositional constituents but propositional differences, and it is also true that philosophical investigations are conceptual investigations, what philosophy needed, Ryle thought, was a means of exhibiting such differences. He took his cue for the method he developed from the work of Russell, whose struggle with the paradoxes resulting in his theory of types had introduced Ryle to a dimension absent in the work of Frege, but omnipresent in Wittgenstein's *Tractatus*, the dimension of sense and nonsense. It was his insistence on the importance of this dimension for work in philosophy that provided the rationale for all of Ryle's work. The method derived from concentrating on this dimension was most clearly articulated in his paper 'Categories', and was programmatically expounded in his inaugural lecture of 1945 entitled 'Philosophical Arguments'.

The central theme of 'Categories' was an attempt to give a general characterisation of what Ryle called 'type trespasses'. In his characterisation of these he made the move which I have said was characteristic of him and which set the tone for much subsequent philosophical work. He shifted, and shifted quite deliberately, from talking about concepts and propositions to talking about sentences and expressions. He shifted, that is, into the semantic or linguistic idiom.

I do not think it is difficult to see why he made this move. It was not that he came to distrust the idea that philosophical investigations are conceptual investigations. His worry was that concepts cannot be made the subjects of true or false propositions. While they make contributions to propositions they are not parts of propositions that can be taken out for investigation. But this, he saw, was manifestly not true of the sentences in which propositions are expressed. 'It is patent', he argued, 'that in a certain sense sentences contain parts; for two sentences can be partially similar and partially dissimilar.' His idea was that while we cannot get at concepts neat, so to speak, we can, nevertheless, learn about them in a systematic way by an examination of the expressions which house them. Parallelling Frege's function and argument distinction with a distinction between expressions, Ryle talked about parts of sentences as 'sentence frames' and 'sentence factors'. From these overtly linguistic items he proceeded to derive the notions of 'propositional frames' and 'propositional factors', and from this derivation in turn he sought to show that certain seeming propositions are not genuine propositions at all; for the sentences in which they are expressed do not make sense. 'When a sentence is (not true or false but) nonsensical or absurd' he argued 'we say that it is absurd because at least one ingredient expression is not of the right type to be coupled in that way with other ingredient expressions in it' (Ryle, 1938, p. 179). This was why he thought that we could achieve by moving into a semantic or linguistic idiom what we could not achieve without doing so. It is not only, as he sometimes put it, prudent to philosophise in a semantic idiom; on his account there would be no other way of philosophising. The only way in which we can talk about concepts is by talking about the ways in which they are expressed. Ryle recognised that there might be a danger in that we might take ourselves to be talking grammar, but he thought that that danger had to be faced, for if we tried to talk not about the expressions themselves, but about what they signify our position would be quite hopeless. The reason for this he argued, is that 'there is not and cannot be any universal title for all the *significata* of expressions, since if there were such a title all these *significata* would be one and the same type' (Ryle, 1938, p. 180–181). This is how he diagnosed what was wrong with Descartes' and Locke's doctrine of ideas as well as Russell's theory of terms.

Now this last passage is, I think, very revealing. I argued in chapter one that what is in fact at bottom wrong with the Lockean terminology of ideas has nothing specifically to do with ideas as such but that it suffers from the defect that any itemising account of the nature of judgment suffers from i.e. it cannot capture the unity of judgment. We have seen that Ryle not only was aware of this problem but saw it as crucial. Consequently his move into the semantic or linguistic idiom, coupled with his modification of the doctrine of types, must have been seen by him as providing a resolution to it. The consideration of linguistic expressions, unlike the consideration of ideas, must have seemed to him to provide a means of resolving it. The question is, 'How were they supposed to do this? Why should talking about language enable us to understand the unity of judgments or the unity of propositions when talking about ideas cannot?' It is tempting to paraphrase a remark from the *Tractatus* by asking 'Does not Ryle's concern with linguistic items correspond to the study of ideas which philosophers used to consider essential to philosophy of logic. Only in most cases they got themselves entangled in unessential psychological investigations, and with Ryle's method there is an analogous risk of getting involved in unessential linguistic or grammatical problems.' What is there about Ryle's concentration on linguistic items which was supposed to allow it to escape these difficulties?

The answer, I think, can only be that he was interested in linguistic expressions only in the background of a theory of types or categories. And on Ryle's view this could only mean that we speak about linguistic items in philosophy with a view to assessing them, not in the dimension of truth and falsity, but in the dimension of sense and nonsense. Linguistic items are important because they are the only items which feature in that dimension. While propositions or thoughts are what are true or false, they can neither make sense nor be nonsensical. The only subjects for these epithets are linguistic expressions. When we speak of parts of sentences (linguistic items) in the background of the sense/nonsense dimension, we are enabled to do what we cannot do by speaking about parts of propositions. In other words Ryle's doctrine of categories of linguistic expression was brought in to play the role that I have argued Russell allocated to 'denoting' in *The Principles of Mathematics*, and which he later thought he could abandon once the notion of the variable had been sorted out. It enabled him to itemise and theorise about propositions without destroying their unity. What is said could in this way survive its own analysis. The investigation of the constituents of propositions could, on this account, only be pursued in a linguistic idiom.

The point that I want to stress is that despite his clear recognition of the problem to which I have argued Frege and Wittgenstein thought that there could be no theoretical solution, Ryle's thinking is much closer in this respect to that of Russell who thought that he had provided such a solution. We have seen that Russell's solution was to regard the unrestricted variable as basic, and to use the technique of the theory of descriptions to eliminate the 'denoting terms' of the *Principles*. This, however, still left him with the problem of the paradoxes. Although the variable had to be considered as unrestricted, nevertheless certain interpretations of it resulted in contradiction and some device was needed to avoid these. The device which Russell invented was the theory of types of terms. While the variable symbolized ambiguously any term, terms themselves still needed to be typified or categorised otherwise paradoxes ensue. The theory of 'denoting terms', seemingly abolished by the unrestricted variable and the theory of descriptions, was smuggled back in by the theory of types. The trouble is that any theory of types automatically breaks its own rules. If we are to learn anything from it, it needs to be taken with Frege's pinch of salt. Ryle's 'categories' were meant to overcome these difficulties. Since there is no difficulty in linguistic expressions being made the subject of true or false propositions it should be logically impeccable to categorise these within the dimension of sense and nonsense. This categorisation would be the investigation of propositional constituents, i.e. of concepts, so that in the end conceptual analysis would turn out to be a certain kind of investigation of linguistic items.

With hindsight I do not think that it is difficult to show that this attempt to find subjects for conceptual propositions which would allow conceptual investigations to be a theoretical business will not work. If concepts themselves cannot be made the subjects of true or false propositions, then neither are we going to be able to talk about them by talking about something else instead. The categorisation of linguistic items in the dimension of sense and nonsense can be seen to be a completely circular affair in Ryle's writings. The situation was one in which we were being told in one breath that two sentence factors are of different types if they engender, in the one case sense, and in the other case nonsense, when offered as fillings for a particular sentence frame; while in the next breath we were being offered the fact that two sentence factors are of a different type to explain why one coupling makes sense and the other does not. The fact, for example, that 'Monday sleeps peacefully' does not make sense while 'My wife sleeps peacefully' does, is the only ground we have for saying that 'Monday' and 'My wife' belong to different categories of linguistic expression. But when we ask for some explanation of why the first does not make sense while the second does, we need to invoke the fact that 'Monday' and 'My wife' belong to different categories of expression. Types of filling for sentence frames are explained in terms of the distinction between sense and nonsense and the distinction between sense and nonsense is explained in terms of the distinction between types of filling for sentence frames. What the circularity shows is that the notion of a type of linguistic expression is not doing any real work. All the work is being done by our ability to distinguish sense from nonsense, and in particular our ability to recognise nonsense when we see it.

There are indications throughout Ryle's work that he realised that the solution he provided for the problem of the unity of a proposition, and therefore his account of the nature of concepts and conceptual investigations were inadequate. In his earliest influential paper 'Systematically Misleading Expressions', for example, having explored the way in which certain expressions can mislead, by utilising a batch of *reductio ad absurdum* arguments, a tool which in his hands became the main philosophical weapon, he ends with the question 'but what are the tests of absurdity?' The argument of his paper 'Categories' was meant to give the theoretical background in which the deployment of *reductio ad absurdum* arguments had more than just an *ad hominem* appeal, and his inaugural lecture 'Philosophical Arguments' was meant to develop a conception of philosophy, a programme for philosophy, from the power of *reductio ad absurdum* arguments deployed within the framework of a doctrine of categories.

Here there begins a new sort of enquiry, the deliberate attempt to discover the real (as distinct from the naively anticipated) logical powers of ideas. The logical absurdities, which betray the original type confusions give an intellectual shock and set a theoretical problem, the problem of determining with method

and with definitive checks the rules governing the correct manipu-
lation of concepts. This task can be metaphorically described as
the charting of the logical powers of ideas (Ryle, 1945, p. 201).

The new method was to be given its first major exemplification
in *The Concept of Mind*.

To the best of my knowledge no one has commented on the
extraordinary title of Ryle's book. It should have been thought
incredible that a philosopher who had concentrated so much of
his efforts on the difficulties which ensue if we seek to make
concepts into the subjects of propositions should make a particular concept the subject, not of a single proposition, but of a
multitude of propositions, a whole book, and to give the book
as a title the very kind of phrase that causes all the trouble.

For Ryle, like Russell, but unlike Frege and Wittgenstein, the
problem of the unity of a proposition, i.e. the problem of the
nature of concepts needed a theoretical solution from which
would evolve a new method in philosophy. While Russell's
solution involved a conception of the variable which, *via* the
theory of descriptions, ultimately permitted him to develop the
method of 'logical functions', saved from the paradox by a
theory of types, Ryle, by making linguistic expressions, about
which we have no logical difficulty in saying true (or false)
things, his subject-matter, thought that by setting what we say
about such expressions in the dimension of sense and nonsense
he could utilise the power of *reductio ad absurdum* arguments to
map relations between concepts. What could not be done
directly could be done indirectly by an appropriate consideration of linguistic expressions. For both Russell and Ryle a
theoretical problem generated a theoretical solution out of which
emerged a conception of philosophy as a special kind of theoretical enterprise.

It was not very long, however, before the theory began to
look very shaky indeed. The idea of categories of expression
which was at its centre was soon being used by Ryle in a highly
untheoretical way. In the early chapters of *The Concept of Mind*
the apparatus of 'sentence factors' and 'sentence frames', 'prop-

ositional factors' and 'propositional frames' had already been dropped and indeed the idea of discovering categories of expression as such had given way to the idea of 'category mistakes'. Although this idea was there introduced in terms of disarmingly homely examples, such as Oxford University being confused with one of its colleges, and team spirit being thought of as a component of a team, it is nevertheless pretty clear that the idea of category mistakes has in the end no more content than the *reductio ad absurdum* arguments which purportedly reveal them. Ryle himself later remarked, again disarmingly, that the term category is worth taking pains with 'not for the usual reason, namely that there exists an exact, professional way of using it, in which, like a skeleton-key, it will turn all our locks for us; but rather for the unusual reason that there is an inexact, amateurish way of using it in which, like a coal-hammer, it will make a satisfactory knocking noise on doors which we want opened to us' (Ryle, 1953, p. 7). The programme of philosophising within a theoretical framework which required that its subject should be linguistic expressions, and the aim of which was to explain why some combinations of expressions make sense while others do not was, I think, gradually dropped. The concept of thinking itself, the concept central to the Cartesian view of the mind which *The Concept of the Mind* was designed to demolish, proved to be recalcitrant to any such treatment.

Ryle's doctrine of categories was, then, a theory about expressions, pieces of language. It was a theory that was designed to explain what Wittgenstein in the *Tractatus* claimed could not be said but could only be shown, viz. the logical form of a proposition. In order to say what the logical form of a proposition is we cannot, it seems, escape the requirement that we speak about the constituents of propositions. Any attempt to do that, however, results in nonsense. What Ryle tried to do was to use the fact that such attempts result in nonsense to generate a philosophical programme. If we could provide an account of the distinction between sense and nonsense, i.e. if we could provide a general account of what makes sense and what does not, we would have at our disposal a way of characterising the logical form of propositions which would bypass the impossible requirement of referring to propositional constituents. Since we can say what sense and nonsense are, in particular since we can say what nonsense is, we can in the end say what Wittgenstein thought could only be shown. What the demise of his doctrine of categories shows us is that we miss the distinction between sense and nonsense when we try to say what nonsense is.

I think that this point can best be brought out by considering once more the second of Frege's three *Grundlagen* principles: never to ask for the meaning of a word in isolation, but only in the context of a proposition. The first thing that we notice when we consider this in the light of Ryle's views is that unlike Frege's other two principles it is overtly linguistic or semantic. Frege's claim, we should recall, was that if we fail to observe this principle we should invariably break his first principle 'always to separate sharply the psychological from the logical, the subjective from the objective'. The idea that Frege pressed is that, from a logical point of view, linguistic expressions, words, are not important in their own right but are only important in terms of what they mean. If we seek to discover that by considering them in isolation we shall be obliged to search for some item or object which is their meaning, and this will almost certainly push theorists of meaning into some form of psychologism. It will rapidly become clear that anything that we might ordinarily call an object is unsuitable as a candidate for the meaning of a word, and we shall be led to cast around for extraordinary items to do the job. Descartes' and Locke's ideas were of course the natural candidates for such a job since they were, at least in part, invented to perform it. So if we ask for the meaning of a word in isolation; if, that is, from a logical point of view we concentrate on linguistic expressions as such, we shall fail to distinguish the logical from the psychological. It is best when we are thinking about words and their meanings to take Wittgenstein's advice in the *Philosophical Investigations* and not to ask for their meaning but to ask for their use. Not because the meaning of a word is not some object or other but something else, namely its use, but rather that from a logical point of view words as such are unimportant except in so far as they can be used to say something. Wittgenstein's advice is a way of putting Frege's second principle, the so called contextual principle.

Now to accuse Ryle of missing these points might seem a little bit like trying to teach your grandmother to suck eggs. It will be pointed out that the naming theory of meaning was a theory which Ryle himself did as much as any philosopher to demolish, dubbing it with his customary brusqueness the 'Fido' Fido view of words and language; and that it was the central theme of *The Concept of Mind* that such a theory of meaning lay behind the myth of the ghost in the machine. Moreover, we have already seen how keenly Ryle was alert to the problem of making propositional constituents themselves the subjects of propositions. Yet, despite all this, I think that it remains true that Ryle's doctrine of categories does, nevertheless, flout Frege's second principle. The point of it was to give an account of how certain combinations of linguistic expressions make sense while certain other combinations failed to make sense. To allocate an expression to a category is to give the rules which govern its use. To do so we are obliged to make linguistic expressions *when considered in the dimension of sense and nonsense* the subjects of propositions. We are obliged, that is, to say that the linguistic expression 'Monday' is governed by rules that are broken in the sentence 'Monday sleeps peacefully' but which are not broken in the sentence 'Monday is the first working day of the week', whereas the linguistic expression 'My wife' is governed by rules which are broken in the sentence 'My wife is the first working day of the week' but which are not broken in the sentence 'My wife sleeps peacefully'. If we are trying to explain in this way why in each case we have a sentence which makes sense and a sentence which does not, then we are obliged to consider the expressions 'Monday' and 'My wife' as independently being governed by rules wich we can then notice to be flouted when these expressions are conjoined with others. But when we are considering linguistic expressions with a view to discovering which combinations of them make sense and which do not this is precisely what we cannot do. To consider linguistic expressions with this aim in mind is to ask about what is said by means of them. Divorced from such a consideration there is nothing to consider from the point of view of what makes sense and what does not. If we should only ask for the meaning of a word in the context of a proposition then there can be no such thing as the rules governing the use of an expression which will show that it is meaningful in some sentences and not in others. Consequently, while it is true that linguistic expressions as such can indeed be made the subject of true (and false) propositions, this is just not the case when they are being considered, as Wittgenstein put it in the *Tractatus*, as thoughts made perceptible to the senses. Ryle's 'linguistic expressions considered in the dimension of sense and nonsense' are just that. His doctrine of categories of linguistic expression was at odds with his oft reiterated Frege-derived, contention that concepts, parts of propositions, are not so much propositional constituents as propositional differences.

SIX

TRUTH AND MEANING

The responses to the problem of the unity of the proposition that I have so far discussed have alternated between the insistence that there can be no theoretical or technical solution (Frege and Wittgenstein.) and the attempts to produce a technical or theoretical solution (Russell and Ryle). I shall shortly be considering Wittgenstein's continued response to the problem in his later work, in particular the *Philosophical Investigations*, but for clarity of exposition it is appropriate at this point to discuss a view which in recent years has attracted a vast amount of attention, and indeed is in danger of becoming the current orthodoxy of the philosophical journals. I refer to the programme for constructing a theory of meaning proposed by Donald Davidson. The programme is presented in a variety of papers now collected in a volume entitled *Inquiries into Truth and Interpretation*.

It is clear from the outset that a recognition of what I have been calling Bradley's problem is a principal philosophical motivation behind Davidson's writings. Over and over again he reminds us of the bankruptcy of what I have called the itemising account of propositions which he, like Bradley, considers to be at the heart of the empiricists' failure to deal adequately with language and thought. A great deal of the seductiveness of his work comes from his ability to spot it at work even in the writings of those who have done most to discredit empiricism.

The problem as Davidson sees it, is to hold on to the idea that a theory of meaning 'must give an account of how the meanings of sentences depend upon the meanings of words', while denying that such an account has to *begin* with the meaning of words. In so far as this sets the problem for Davidson, thus far are his endeavours identical to those of Russell and Ryle. We have seen how the idea of denoting in the *Principles of Mathematics* was an idea introduced to do just that job, since the capacity to denote was possessed only by terms which do not occur as terms in propositions. For Russell, the meaning of sentences depended upon the meaning of the words in them, i.e. the terms for which they stood, but we only had a sentence expressing a proposition when one of those terms did not occur as a term. The importance of denoting was precisely that it was a capacity possessed by the meaning of a word (a term) but which could not be brought out by giving the meaning of a word, since all attempts to do that inevitably ended by destroying the unity of the proposition. Davidson, like Russell, is concerned with the break-up of propositions while recognising that the most natural notion of analysis, when applied to propositions, destroys their unity. We have seen in the last chapter how this problem was the source of most of Ryle's work, and how it forced him to adopt a linguistic approach with which he was never altogether happy.

Davidson's solution to the problem, while it is bolstered by an array of logical technicalities is, at heart, brilliant in its simplicity. First of all he encourages us to bring to the centre of the picture Frege's second principle, or, if you like, Wittgenstein's idea of an expression or a symbol. We should return, he argues, to the insight that the only sense in which it is true to say that words have meaning is in 'the ontologically neutral sense of making a systematic contribution to the meaning of the sentences in which they occur.' He then, and this we shall see is the decisive move, extends the principle. 'Frege said that only in the context of a sentence does a word have meaning; in the same vein we might add that only in the context of a language

does a sentence (and therefore a word) have meaning' (Davidson, 1967, p. 22).

The lesson which Davidson draws from this extended version
of Frege's insight, however, bears no relation to the lesson drawn
by Frege and Wittgenstein. Both of these, we have seen, concluded that the attempt to theorise, i.e. to produce a body of
organised truths about the meaning of words (or sentences), is
necessarily doomed to failure. Davidson's solution, on the other
hand, is in principle much more like Ryle's in one central
respect, although it is poles apart from it in detail. I shall argue
in fact that the description 'poles apart' is entirely accurate since
Davidson's theory turns out to be, in the relevant respects, a
straightforward assertion of what Ryle was concerned to
deny.

Ryle, we have seen, located the problem in philosophers'
attempts to talk directly about meaning. He thought that we
could achieve the desired result by speaking indirectly about it,
by speaking, that is, not about the parts of propositions but
about parts of sentences; not about logical items but about
linguistic items, with the important *proviso* that we should speak
about them in the dimension not of truth and falsity but of sense
and nonsense. Davidson's solution, although technically very
different, is in the same vein. If our problem stems from our
efforts to give the meaning of a word or a sentence, and yet it
turns out that any attempt to postulate meanings 'nets nothing',
then the right thing to do is not to seek to talk about meanings,
since we cannot, but rather to talk about something else which
will have the same effect; which will, so to speak, be as good as
talking about meanings. We must seek to achieve indirectly
what we cannot achieve directly.

We can begin, he suggests, by eliminating talk about the
meaning of sentences. Instead of saying '*s* means *m*' we can
simply say '*s* means that *p*' where what replaces *p* is a sentence.
If the 'means that' gives the impression that all of our old
problems will come flooding back we can eliminate it and still
achieve the same effect.

The theory will have done its work if it provides, for every sentence *s* in the language under study, a matching sentence (to replace *p*) that, in some way yet to be made clear, 'gives the meaning of *s*'. One obvious candidate for matching sentence is just *s* itself . . . As a final bold step let us try treating the position occupied by '*p*' extensionally: to implement this, sweep away the obscure 'means that', provide the sentence that replaces '*p*' with a proper sentential connective, and supply the description that replaces '*s*' with its own predicate. The plausible result is   (T) *s* is T if and only if *p*.

It is the final 'bold step', of course, that gives us the programme for constructing a theory of meaning which, while necessarily indirect, is supposed to be none the less effective. No more is required of a theory of meaning, Davidson argues, than that 'it places enough restrictions on the predicate 'is T' to entail all sentences got from schema T when "*s*" is replaced by a structural description of a sentence of *L* and "*p*" by that sentence' (Davidson, 1967, p. 23). And since Schema T is instantly recognisable as Tarski's material adequacy condition for a definition of truth we arrive at the conclusion that a theory of meaning is obtained by discovering the restrictions that are placed upon the predicate '. . . is true'. A theory of truth, when correctly understood, is a theory of meaning.

When we have become confident of this line of reasoning a programme for philosophical analysis unfolds. The 'T' schema gives us a way of testing whatever structural analysis of a particular sentence we come up with, and since structural analysis, in Davidson's eyes, is just another way of talking about logical form, philosophy has worked its way back to the idea of analysis that Russell sought to defend. As Davidson himself acknowledges, 'making a systematic account of truth central in empirical semantics is in a way merely a matter of stating old goals more sharply'. We know, let us say, that we have the correct structural analysis or logical form of 'The king of France is bald' in – shall we say – 'Something is France's king, and only one thing is France's king, and whatever is France's king is bald' because we know that this is true if and only if the king of France is bald. We equally know that we do not have the correct structural analysis or logical form of 'Margaret Thatcher is a good woman' in 'Margaret Thatcher is good and Margaret Thatcher is a woman' because we know that this is not true if and only if Margaret Thatcher is a good woman. While Russell used restrictions on the predicate ' ... is true' to get at logical form under a conception of logical form which required items of meaning (terms), what, in effect, Davidson does is to agree with the method while denying the need for such items. What he thinks enables him to do this is his extension of Frege's contextual principle beyond sentences to language as such. A holistic view of meaning allows him to maintain truth as a test of form while dispensing with meanings.

It is worthwhile bringing out in a little more detail why Davidson thinks that this is so just because it is this aspect of his work which has most bearing on the problem with which I am concerned. The constant defence and reiteration of Tarski's definition of truth in terms of satisfaction is really peripheral. From the point of view of the ability of a theory of meaning to overcome the difficulties inherent in an itemising account, the definition of a truth predicate is of secondary importance. Davidson himself points out that, on his view, we would know that we had a theory of meaning for a language if we had a theory which for every sentence of the language entails a T-sentence, even if we had no notion whatsoever of the predicate which attaches to the structural description of a sentence in the statement of the T-sentence. If for every sentence 's' of a language we knew that it was Q if and only if p then we would have a theory of meaning for that language whatever predicate ' ... is Q' turned out to be. It would be enough that some predicate attaches to the structural description under the condition of the T-sentence. It was meant to be an independent discovery, or incidental bonus, that any such predicate would indeed, if Tarski is correct, be the truth predicate. It is not so much that a theory of truth enables us to repair the deficiencies in an itemising account, rather that the extension of the contextual principle from sentences to language as a whole does this, and that such an extension turns out to be indiscernably different from a theory of truth.

The development of Frege's contextual principle from 'Only in the context of a sentence does a word have meaning' to 'Only in the context of a language does a sentence (and therefore a word) have meaning' enables Davidson to escape the itemising problem just because the idea of providing a matching sentence for every sentence of a language structurally described relieves him of the worry about a language containing potentially an infinite number of sentences. If we could make sense of an itemising account then the device of recursion would take care of that problem for it provides us with a means of constructing an infinite number of sentences from a finite stock of items. If we cannot make sense of an itemising account, however, the problem remains. The extension of the contextual principle, Davidson thinks, solves the problem. If we had a theory which enabled us, *no matter how*, to provide a matching sentence for a structural description of every sentence in a language, i.e. for each of the potentially infinite number of sentences, then the fact that that number is potentially infinite would no longer be a worry; we can achieve, by providing matching sentences, what we wanted to achieve by a recursion over items of meaning, so we have no theoretical need to worry about items of meaning. The theory of meaning, as Davidson puts it, can dispense with meanings.

In dispensing with meanings, however there is no need to throw the baby out with the bath-water. The structural analysis of sentences into the familiar terms of logical theory can still have a role, and it may prove not only indispensable but also sufficient. The machinery can still be used in a climate free from itemising anxiety. Davidson thinks of the research going ahead in the following fashion. First of all the hypothesis is advanced that some T-sentence is true. A theory of the restrictions on the truth predicate is devised which would explain why the T-sentence is true. This theory is then tested against further T-sentences which would no doubt lead to the modification of the theory and so on. 'The theory', he tells us, 'will, of course, contain a recursion on a concept like that of satisfaction or reference.'

> But these notions we must treat as theoretical constructs whose function is exhausted in stating the truth conditions for sentences. Similarly, for that matter, for the logical form attributed to sentences, and the whole machinery of terms, predicates, connectives and quantifiers. None of this is open to direct confrontation with the evidence. It makes no sense, on this approach, to complain that a theory comes up with the right truth conditions time after time, but has the logical form (or deep structure) wrong (Davidson, 1977, p. 222–223).

We might put Davidson's point in the following way. Philosophers have been accustomed from the beginning of the century, largely due to the work of Russell and Frege, to seek to determine the logical form of sentences by using the now familiar logical apparatus largely devised by them. The programme, although it never quite fell into disrepute, nevertheless generated difficulties because of the seemingly insoluble problems associated with the business of referring to the parts of sentences or propositions indispensable to the task of giving an account of logical form or structure. Such parts could not in the end be referred to independently of the sentences or propositions of which they were parts. Words turn out only to have meaning in the context of sentences. The problem is cured by a form of theoretical homeopathy. An extra dose of the principle that causes the trouble effects a cure for it. If a sentence only has meaning in the context of all the sentences of a language, then the initial talk about parts of sentences, i.e. the original talk about logical form, takes on the role of an heuristic device which enables us to match characterisations of sentences to sentences themselves. The benefit which accrues is that what was a liability for a supposed theory of how parts of a sentence or proposition go to make up that sentence or proposition is not *ipso facto* a liability for an heuristic device (a theoretical construct), the only purpose of which is to enable us to match characterisations of sentences with sentences. In fact it turns out to be no liability at all. The extension of the contextual principle to the meanings of sentences extricates the programme from difficulties which had come to seem ineradicable.

It should now be clear why I regard Davidson's views as being at once similar in principle to Ryle's and yet at the same time poles apart. Both are interested in the investigation of meaning, and both recognise that the context principle acts as a bar to earlier conceptions of logical form if the tests for correctness of logical form need to be conducted within the dimension of truth and falsity. However, whereas Ryle thought that this showed that we needed another testing ground, and argued that it could only be the dimension of sense and nonsense, Davidson seeks to remain within the old testing ground by extending the contextual principle.

Davidson is of course aware that using our intuitions about truth to arrive at a conception of logical form eventually drove Russell to despair, or, if it is not the same thing, at least to his theory of types, when he discovered that there are occasions when our intuitions about truth get us nowhere whatsoever, i.e. that there are certain occasions when whatever direction they lead us in we end with paradox; and that Tarski himself, from whom the 'T' schema is borrowed, came to the conclusion that the attempt to define truth for ordinary languages will inevitably end in the mire of the semantic paradoxes. So far as I can determine he has nothing to say about these problems, short of urging that we are justified in carrying on with the programme 'without having disinfected this particular source of conceptual anxiety'. The anxiety, however, should be seen as an anxiety about the programme as a whole and not just about the application of Tarski's convention (T) in certain areas. For if its source cannot be disinfected we have grounds for believing that while restrictions on a truth predicate may be capable of revealing many things, they cannot be used to reveal logical form, i.e. they cannot be used as a test for the logical structure of sentences, even when we consider restrictions on the truth predicate in the background of a holistic conception of language. While it must be conceded that an heuristic device or theoretical construct is inappropriately subject to criticisms that are entirely appropriate to claims of discovery, nevertheless, given that the goal for which the device was devised has not yet been reached, it still remains a subject for scrutiny.

It is, no doubt, both disarming and encouraging to be told that our familiar ways of breaking up sentences into 'words, meanings of words, reference, and satisfaction' are immune from a particular kind of detailed criticism just because they are only to be thought of as 'posits we need to implement a theory of truth' and that '[t]hey serve this purpose without needing independent confirmation or empirical basis': for with regard to heuristic devices anything goes so long as they serve their heuristic purpose; in this case that of enabling us to match characterisations of sentences with sentences. Our confidence may, however, begin to slump again when it dawns on us that we have not the ghost of a notion of what other device, or set of devices, might be used to achieve the same end. Moreover, 'independent confirmation' might sound the same as 'empirical basis', but where logical apparatus is concerned it had better not be treated as the same. If the only heuristic device we can think of for achieving a particular goal cannot be prevented from generating contradictions then this is not a reason for excusing it on the grounds that it is, after all, only an heuristic device. On the contrary, it provides a reason for questioning the goal towards which it was thought to be the best, if not the only, means. From the point of view of Davidson's programme for building a theory of meaning, what this in effect means is that it gives us grounds for questioning the extension of the context principle. It should make us suspicious of his holism. Suspicions about holism, in turn, engender suspicions about Davidson's ideas about the way truth is related to meaning.

The best way I know to bring these suspicions into sharp focus is to ask about the nature of the truth predicate in the T schema. If we could conclude with Ramsey that any such predicate is always eliminable then we should also have succeeded in casting doubt upon Davidson's extended version of the context principle; for we would have shown that the only conceptual tool capable of being employed within his version of an holistic conception of meaning is worthless, viz. the idea of a T-sentence. Without a truth predicate there would be no such sentences. However, I share the widely held view that truth as a predicate is not always eliminable. But this should not prevent us from concentrating on those cases in which Ramsey showed it could be eliminated, and from asking ourselves the question 'When is it proper to think of truth as a predicate and when is it not?' More specifically, is it appropriate to think of truth as a predicate when we are trying to become clear about logical form or logical structure, given, that is, that we think of becoming clear about logical form or structure as discovering the way in which parts of a sentence contribute to what is said by means of it?

It should not be denied, of course, that there are plenty of occasions when it is perfectly appropriate to think of truth as a predicate. To say that someone has said something true is in any ordinary way of speaking to have said something about, i.e. to have predicated something of, what that person said. I find it quite extraordinary that so much of the debate about truth in recent years should have concerned this point. In the sciences, in the law, and in our ordinary everyday discourse, of course truth is a predicate. It cannot but be a matter of concern to us whether what is said by lawyers, scientists etc. is true or whether it is false. But if our concern is with logic the case is different. If we grant that we are concerned in logic with what is true and what is false, if we are concerned, that is, with propositions, thoughts, or sentences in which something is said, it should equally be granted that we are not concerned with whether what is said is actually true or actually false. It is just because logic is concerned with the true and the false, with, as Frege put it, the laws of truth, that there can be no room for a truth predicate in logic. The fact that we are concerned with an area in which there can be no room for a truth predicate is what distinguishes logical from other concerns. If we were concerned with anything else, with shoes or ships or sealing-wax, then we cannot do without a truth predicate for we wish to find out truths about these things. But when truth itself is our concern it cannot be truths that we are looking for, and if we tried to introduce a truth predicate into our accounts it would just cancel itself out.

This idea that in logic a truth *predicate* is redundant is part and parcel of the idea that considerations about truth can be used to reveal logical form. It lies behind the idea of a truth function. In the propositional calculus, for example, it belongs to the idea of such a calculus that its elements are true or false, so that when we say of a complex proposition that it is a function of the truth of the elementary propositions it contains we mean only that there is no more to the truth or falsity of the complex proposition than the truth or falsity of the elementary propositions. Given those there is no further question of truth. The truth of the complex proposition is not something over and above the truth of the elementary propositions. That is what we mean when we say that a complex or non-elementary proposition is a truth function. If we try to treat the truth of the complex proposition as something over and above the truth of the elementary propositions it contains then the notion of a truth function is destroyed. Both Wittgenstein and Frege saw that it equally collapsed if we try to treat ' ... is true' as a predicate of elementary propositions. This is why Wittgenstein maintained that elementary propositions are truth functions of themselves. From the point of view of a calculus of propositions, the truth or falsity of an elementary proposition is not something over and above the elementary proposition, i.e. it is not something that can be seen to hold of it, any more than the truth or falsity of a complex proposition is something over and above the truth or falsity of the elementary propositions it contains. The point is that the idea of a truth function would be destroyed altogether if we allowed truth to be a predicate in the calculus. Truth functions are not functions proper. Truths and falsehoods are not themselves true or false. In the calculus of propositions, while the elements are truths or falsehoods there is no requirement that truth be predicated of them. In the working of the calculus a truth predicate is redundant just because all predicates are redundant.

When we understand the way in which truth can be made to reveal form by means of the idea of a truth function, we begin to understand why Frege was so appalled at the reception given to his introduction of the idea by means of his invention of the conditional stroke. The following passage indicates why I do not think that 'appalled' is too strong a word.

> If there are two thoughts only four cases are possible: 1. the first is true and likewise the second; 2. the first is true, the second false; 3. the first is false, the second true; 4. both are false./ Now if the third of these cases does not obtain then the relation I have designated by the *conditional stroke* obtains.... It is now 28 years since I gave this definition. I believed at the time that I only had to mention it and everyone else would immediately know more about it than I did. And now after more than a quarter of a century has elapsed, the great majority of mathematicians have no inkling of the matter, and the same goes for logicians. What pig-headedness. This way academics have of behaving reminds me of nothing so much as that of an ox confronted by a new gate: it gapes, it bellows, it tries to squeeze by sideways, but going through it – that might be dangerous (Frege, 1969, p. 187).

Frege thought that the reaction to his idea of the conditional stroke was largely due to the fact that people were inclined to think that indicating that the third of the possibilities does not obtain must have something to do with the content of the thoughts in question, whereas he insisted that what was important about the idea was that the content of the thoughts has nothing to do with the matter. When we are operating at the level of Frege's conditional stroke we are not interested in the contents of thoughts. It follows from this that we are not interested in predicates (or functions proper), and most importantly for the point I am trying to make, it follows that we are not interested in a truth predicate. We will go wrong if we try to read the 'is true' and the 'is false' of Frege's 'the first is false and the second true' as indicating something that is predicated of the first and the second in the sense that the first falls under the concept ' ... is false' and the second falls under the concept ' ... is true'. In explaining the notion of a truth function, i.e. in explaining the conditional stroke, while we may find ourselves saying things like 'A thought (or a proposition) is whatever is true or false' it would be quite wrong to think of this as meaning the same as 'A thought is whatever falls under the concept of truth or the concept of falsity.' If we are dealing with truth functions, i.e. if we are trying to understand Frege's conditional stroke, truth cannot itself be considered as part of the content of what is truth-functionally related, i.e. it cannot be thought of as part of the content of a thought. This is how we should understand the idea that in logic a truth predicate is redundant.

Essentially the same point is made by Wittgenstein at 136 of the *Philosophical Investigations* in the course of discussing the idea of the general form of propositions.

> Now it looks as if the definition – a proposition is whatever can be true or false – determined what a proposition was, by saying: what fits the concept of 'true', or what the concept 'true' fits is a proposition. So it is as if we had a concept of true and false which we could use to determine what is and what is not a proposition. What *engages* with the concept of truth (as with a cogwheel), is a proposition./ But this is a bad picture. It is as if one were to say 'The king in chess is *the* piece that one can check.' But this can mean no more than in our game of chess we only check the king (Wittgenstein, 1953, p. 52).

Now in saying that there are occasions when ' ... is true' can be considered as a predicate, and occasions when it cannot, it may seem that I am really only echoing what Davidson himself admits, for he also maintains that 'correspondence and redundancy theories do not necessarily conflict'. The moral I draw from this, however, is quite different from the one Davidson draws. The moral I wish to draw is, once again Frege's.

> Just let someone try to give an account [of the conditional stroke] in which the thought itself plays a bigger role and it will probably turn out that what has been added from the thought is at bottom quite superfluous, and that one has only succeeded in complicating the issue, or that the antecedent and consequent are not sentences proper, neither being such as to express a thought (Frege, 1969, p. 185).

In the light of this passage we might notice that the cases in which the so called redundancy theory of truth is said to come to grief are precisely those in which the predicate ' ... is true' is not attached to what Frege calls a thought. Frege, like Ramsey, noticed that while '"S is P" is true' is logically equivalent to 'S is P', 'What Aristotle said is true' does not appear to be reducible to 'What Aristotle said'. Wanting what he said about truth to have complete generality Ramsey tried to find ways of showing that this appearance was deceptive. It is now generally recognised that he was not successful in this. But perhaps that was the wrong strategem. If we hold on to the idea that those cases in which the truth predicate cannot be eliminated are just those cases in which truth is not predicated of what Frege called a thought or a judgeable content, then we might be in a position to see why a redundancy theory and a correspondence theory might not after all be competitors.

Whenever we seek to predicate truth of a thought we fail; the prediction becomes redundant. On the other hand, we can succeed in predicating truth of subjects other than thoughts. In 'What Aristotle said is true' ' ... is true ' is a genuine predicate just because 'What Aristotle said' does not express a thought (it is not something that can be substituted for the p's and q's of the propositional calculus). When truth is genuinely predicated of something, paradoxical though this may sound, what it is predicated of is not something which is 'either true or false', in the terms of calculus of propositions, i.e. in the sense in which judgeable contents, propositions, or thoughts are said to be either true or false. The moral that should be drawn from this is the moral that Frege himself drew. When we are seeking the laws of truth, i.e. when we are doing logic, we of necessity have to dispense with truth as a predicate since, whenever it is predicated, what it is predicated of would not be a concern of logic.

Frege's moral should be seen as having no exceptions. It holds good even of those cases in which we are seeking to get clear about the structure of propositions in which, unlike the propositional calculus, the idea of predication is central. Once more Frege's way of doing this makes the point clear. It is only after the introduction of the conditional stroke that he considered that the 'need arises to analyse a thought into parts none of which are thoughts'. That is to say, it is only after the introduction of the conditional stroke that we need to deploy the distinction between concept and object, or the distinction between unsaturated and saturated parts of thoughts in order to understand the structure of general thoughts. While all thoughts, on his account, divide into a saturated part and an unsaturated part, such a division only needs to be employed in a calculus of thoughts at the point when we seek to understand general thoughts. If this is so, then the process of arriving at an understanding of general thoughts is a process that at no stage requires truth to be predicated of a thought. We begin with two thoughts A and B, we then form the opposite of thought A, we then form the conjunction of that with thought B, we then form the opposite of this conjunction and then generalise by splitting this up into a saturated and an unsaturated part, substituting an indefinitely indicating letter for the saturated part. In this way we have come to an understanding of the logical form of a general proposition, but at no stage have we been required to predicate anything, let alone truth, of a thought. An understanding of the laws of truth does not require anything to be predicated of what can be true or false (Frege, 1969, p. 189).

Having said all this, of course, we are perfectly at liberty to construct a theory of truth, just as we are at liberty to construct a theory of any other predicate. That is to say we were perfectly at liberty to seek to ascertain the conditions under which the predicate is appropriately, i.e. truly predicated. It is likely to be the case that this will turn out to be some form of correspondence theory, but whether it does or not there will be no conflict between the claim that in logic the predicate ' ... is true' is redundant and the defence of a correspondence theory of truth, or, for that matter, any theory of truth whatsoever.

Now it might seem that in allowing that some version of the correspondence theory of truth might well be the correct one I have allowed Davidson all the leeway he needs for the programme he has so forcefully urged. But, in point of fact, I think exactly the opposite. If what I have said about the relationship between the so called redundancy view and the correspondence theory is correct then the fact that in a T-sentence we do have a truth predicate is itself sufficient ground for concluding that what truth is predicated of in that sentence is not a judgeable content. Consequently, whatever structure it can be analysed into will not be a structure that is at all revealing of logical form. The structural description of a sentence that allows truth to be predicated of it will not be a description which brings out the ways in which sentences are truth functionally related. Canonical notation is inappropriately applied to anything that truth can be appropriately predicated of, while of course it is entirely appropriately applied to what Frege called a thought or a judgeable content: that is the job for which it was devised.

At the end of his paper 'True to Facts' Davidson says this about the celebrated Austin/Strawson debate:

> Strawson describes Austin's 'purified version of the correspondence theory of truth' in this way: 'His ... theory is, roughly, that to say that a statement is true is to say that a certain speech episode is related in a certain conventional way to something in the world exclusive of itself.' It is this theory Strawson has in mind when he says 'The correspondence theory

requires, not purification, but elimination'. ... If I am right in
appealing to Tarski's semantical conception of truth we can
defend a theory that almost exactly fits Strawson's description of
Austin's 'purified version of the correspondence theory of truth'.
And this theory deserves, not elimination, but elaboration (Davidson, 1969, p. 53–54).

While I agree with this last remark, we can become clearer as
to why such a correspondence theory properly elaborated
cannot serve as a theory of meaning by asking ourselves what
in such a theory is said to be true. Davidson will encourage us
to consider sentences such as 'Sentence s is true (as English) for
speaker u at time t if and only if p'. Such a sentence is supposed
to contain what he calls a relativised truth predicate. But if we
really were to elaborate the correspondence theory of truth in
Austin's purified way it is not the predicate that needs rela-
tivising but rather what it is predicated of. The predicate we
are interested in is the predicate ' ... is true'. In Austin's version
this predicate attaches to speech episodes, and it is these that
occur with regard to a particular person at a particular place
and time. It should need no argument to show that such items
are not capable of the kind of structural analysis which would,
after the fashion of Tarski, transform a theory of truth from a
series of truisms into something genuinely explanatory of logical
form. While it is plausible to suppose that the sentence 'Snow is
white' can be analysed into the argument 'snow' and the predicate ' ... is white', i.e. that they are sentences correctly analysed
after the canonical model Fa, this is not the case with an utter-
ance. A speech episode, like any episode, is an historical occur
rence, and as such is related in all sorts of ways to other episodes
and other things. When Russell said 'There are negative facts'
what he said caused a riot at Harvard, and it is what he said
that is true (actually in this case I think false). What caused the
riot, while it is related to many things, to the riot, for example,
is not truth functionally related to anything. If the idea of logical
form or structural description is tied to the notion of a truth
function, then the prospects for logical form or structural

descriptions being generated by a truth predicate are bleak indeed. Only if meaningfulness has nothing to do with truth could a theory of truth be a theory of meaning.

SEVEN

AGREEMENT IN JUDGMENTS

In an article which he submitted for publication in the year of his death, but which did not see the light of day until the publication of his *nachlass*, Frege wrote the following.

> How does a child learn to understand grown-ups? Not as if it were already endowed with an understanding of a few words and grammatical constructions, so that all you would need to do would be to explain what it did not understand by means of the linguistic knowledge it already had. In reality of course children are only endowed with a capacity to learn to speak. We must be able to count on a meeting of minds with them just as in the case of animals with whom men can arrive at a mutual understanding (Frege, 1969, p. 271).

The remark belongs with a series of similar remarks some of which we have already considered in chapter three. They concern the difficulties inherent in the task of making clear his division of judgeable contents into a complete and an incomplete part, i.e. into concept and object; difficulties which we have seen arise from the impossibility of saying anything at all about the incomplete or unsaturated parts of such contents. For the most part these remarks have an air of resignation about them, as though Frege were acknowledging that his way of thinking about judgeable contents required him to do something which he could not do if his way of thinking were correct, but that, nevertheless, he remained convinced of its correctness. He therefore resorted to asking his readers to provide the necessary 'pinch of salt' with regard to some of the things he wrote, or urged that they should be prepared to 'meet him half way'. It is as though having painted himself into a corner he nevertheless thought that the paintwork was perfect and that that was the only way in which painting could be done. However, the remark that I have just cited does not convey this impression, and I think it does contain a genuine movement of thought on Frege's part; a movement of thought, however, which Frege did not develop. It is the beginnings of a response to the problem of the unity of a proposition which, I shall argue, was developed by Wittgenstein in his later work. I do not, of course, suggest that Wittgenstein was familiar with this remark.

First of all consider the following passage written by Wittgenstein shortly before he died.

> I want to regard man here as an animal; as a primitive being to which one grants instinct but not ratiocination. As a creature in a primitive state. Any logic good enough for a primitive means of communication needs no apology from us. Language did not emerge from some kind of ratiocination (Wittgenstein, 1969b, p. 62).

Frege asked us to concentrate on the way in which there can be a meeting of minds, and Wittgenstein asked us to concentrate on the idea of a primitive means of communication, where what is meant by 'primitive' gains its content by contrast with the idea of ratiocination. Now if we put these two ideas together this should encourage us to think that the worries about the unity of a judgeable content or proposition can be overcome if we can make clear to ourselves how there can be a meeting of minds which is not the product of ratiocination. Anyone familiar with Wittgenstein's *Philosophical Investigations* will recognise immediately one of the central themes of that work, viz. the importance for an understanding of logic and language of agreement in judgments.

The notion is introduced in the *Philosophical Investigations* in the following way.

> If language is to be a means of communication there must be
> agreement not only in definition but also, queer as this may
> sound, in judgments. This seems to abolish logic but does not do
> so. It is one thing to describe the methods of measurement, and
> another to obtain and state the results of measurement. But what
> we call 'measuring' is partly determined by a constancy in the
> results of measurements (Wittgenstein, 1953, p. 88).

When we consider this passage in the background of the difficulties that the analysis of propositions or judgeable contents generate we see that the attempt to individuate, or identify, or define parts of propositions with the aim of saying something about the parts so identified, individuated or defined, has been given up, and the judgments we actually make have been brought into the foreground. This comes out most clearly when we set it in the background of the discussion which prompted Frege's remark about a meeting of minds, for there the problem about parts of judgeable contents had been formulated as a problem about the nature of definition. In particular it arose out of the difficulties that are involved in giving a definition of the term 'function' as it is used in mathematics.

Shortly before the 'meeting of minds' passage, Frege had been stressing the by now familiar point that 'in the formula language of mathematics an important distinction stands out that lies concealed in verbal language.' It is the distinction with which mathematicians become familiar when they grasp, as they need to, the idea of a function. They need to come to terms with this idea, and they do so, but not as a result of any definition that is given to them by their teachers. In the teaching process definitions are indeed advanced, but once advanced no further use is made of them. Worse than this it invariably transpires that not only is no further use made of them but also that the teacher's way of speaking conflicts with the definition that he has given.

The reason for this, from Frege's point of view, is obvious. The form of a definition requires that what is defined is not a function. To give a definition of a particular function, e.g. a sine function, you would need to produce an expression of the form

'The function "sin( )" ...' and yet the one thing that an expression of that form could not designate is a function. Such expressions would be names of arguments or names of objects and a function is precisely not an argument but what leaves a place open for an argument. This tendency to use 'the definite article to stamp as an object what is a function and hence a non-object' is, Frege maintained, at the heart of most of the contaminations of 'the logical source of knowledge' (Frege, 1969, p. 269). It is essential to the idea of a thought that there are parts of a thought that definition cannot reach. It is because of this that Frege insisted that the learning process relies, and has to rely, on a meeting of minds. What I am suggesting is that the nature of a judgeable content, i.e. how it is made up, can only be made clear *via* a consideration of the actual judgments that we make. What we need to concentrate on if we are to understand how the parts of what is said contribute to what is said are not the parts themselves in an isolation they could never enjoy, but on the way in which we agree in what we say.

We must first of all, however, become clear about the nature of the agreement involved. Not every agreement in judgments will constitute a meeting of minds in the required sense. What kind of agreement in judgments is necessary if language is to be a means of communication? It will be a notion of agreement which goes with the idea of a primitive means of communication, and it will be marked by an absence of ratiocination. It will be of the kind that Frege gestured towards with his phrase 'a meeting of minds'. But what sort of an idea of agreement is that?

Although, as I have said, this is one of the central themes of the *Philosophical Investigations*, there are two other works of Wittgenstein that I think are particularly helpful in bringing out the nature of the agreement involved. These are *On Certainty* and the remarks on Fraser's *Golden Bough*.

On Certainty is not always thought of in relation to this theme of the *Philosophical Investigations*. It was, and continues to be, read after the fashion encouraged by Norman Malcolm, who gained the impression, when Wittgenstein was staying with him at the time he wrote the remarks, that his interest in Moore's 'Defence of Common Sense' and 'Proof of an External World' was an entirely new interest, marking a very belated concern with epistemological questions. Anthony Kenny's book on Wittgenstein has helped to reinforce this view which is now widely accepted. In it he wrote the following:

> Wittgenstein being preoccupied with the theory of meaning was comparatively uninterested in epistemology for much of his life. But his work on the philosophy of mind and the foundations of mathematics naturally overlapped with areas which were the traditional province of epistemologists. Towards the end of his life while staying with Norman Malcolm in Ithaca in 1949 he was stimulated by the study of Moore's articles to begin to write on epistemology (Kenny, 1973, p. 204).

What I wish to suggest is that if we read *On Certainty* in this light we shall be liable to miss the way in which it helps us to get clear about the importance Wittgenstein attached to the notion of agreement in judgments in the *Philosophical Investigations*.

If we take as our cue to the understanding of the kind of agreement in question the absence of ratiocination, then the first thing that has to be said about it is that it is a notion of agreement that will not tolerate the notion of disagreement. People agree about many things and disagree about others. The possibility of disagreement paves the way for the giving of reasons for the judgments we make, paves the way, that is, for ratiocination. It follows, therefore, that to illustrate the kind of agreement in question we shall need to fix on situations in which we cannot make sense of someone disagreeing with a judgment that is made. Now in the nature of the case it is going to be hard to find striking examples of such situations for the simple reason that people do not, by and large, go around saying things which it does not makes sense for anyone else to disagree with. It does not follow from this that such judgments are not made, merely that they are not expressed or insisted upon, and their not being expressed or insisted upon is liable to distract our attention from the fact that they are, nevertheless, made.

The articles by Moore are perfect examples with which to illustrate this point. In 'The Defence of Common Sense' and 'Proof of an External World' Moore brought to our attention things about which we all agree, but more than this, he brought to our attention things about which we could not make sense of anyone disagreeing. If someone seriously were to try to convince us that he thought otherwise we would not know what to make of him. And here we do have to take seriously the 'seriously'.

At a meeting of the *Mind* and Aristotelian Society Moore held up one of his hands and said 'Here is one hand' and holding up his other hand said 'Here is another'. It is impossible to conceive how anyone at that meeting could have disagreed with him. Similarly in 'A Defence of Common Sense' he listed a series of banal propositions with which it is impossible to conceive of anyone disagreeing. Moreover, he pointed out just that, i.e. that everyone does agree about these things. His interest was in the fact that, despite this, many philosophers have nevertheless made claims which obviously conflict with them. He attempted to give a diagnosis of this, and located the trouble in the difficulties of giving an analysis of the propositions the truth of which was not questioned.

Now, whatever the merits of that proposal, it is clear that Moore himself considered the kind of agreement that obtains with regard to his celebrated propositions as a kind of agreement that contrasts with disagreement, for he gestured towards the ratiocination (the difficulties in giving an analysis of what is claimed) which is liable to make philosophers say things which conflict, i.e. which is liable to make them think that there is room for disagreement about such matters. The certainty which he claimed for the propositions which he expressed belongs in the area to which the giving of reasons, ratiocination, also belongs. But now, what if the importance which attaches to the claims that he made derives from the fact that the kind of agreement which they secure is not that kind of agreement at all? What if the certainty they enjoy is not the sort of certainty that can be arrived at by resolving doubts, removing qualms or relieving suspicions? Wittgenstein's remarks about Moore in *On Certainty* were all designed to show that this is indeed so.

First and foremost he criticised Moore for expressing the certainty which attaches to these propositions as a form of knowledge. 'Moore' he said 'has every right to say that he knows these things. Naturally he might be wrong.' In claiming to know that he has never been far from the surface of the earth, for example, he left room for the question 'How do you know?' and as soon as that question is asked, when nothing in the way of justification is forthcoming, this will seem to cast doubt on the proposition. By claiming to know these things Moore made it look as though they are things that are not so much beyond question but things that just are not questioned. He made it look as though they are things which we all take for granted, while remaining things which we perhaps should not take for granted, and particularly not in philosophy. But with regard to Moore's propositions, Wittgenstein urged, the certainty which attaches to them does so not because they are beyond doubt in the sense that we have conclusive reasons for believing them, but rather that they are beyond doubt in that we do not have any notion of what a reason for believing them would be and therefore have no notion of what a reason for doubting them would be either. In other words, they are not propositions that are the province of ratiocination. The certainty we have about them is not a certainty that is 'still struggling', it is the 'comfortable certainty' that might be possessed by a primitive being which had instinct but not ratiocination. Rightly conceived, Wittgenstein thought, Moore's defence of common sense is not so much a defence of common knowledge (what every schoolboy knows) but of what might be called common understanding. It brings to our attention 'a lot of empirical propositions that we affirm without special testing; propositions, that is, which have a peculiar logical role in the system of our empirical propositions' (Wittgenstein, 1969b, p. 20).

The way in which we agree about them also has the effect of preventing the idea of agreement with reality from having any clear application in their case. It prevents us from sensibly asking how we know that they agree with reality. This is why the kind of agreement in question leaves no room for disagreement. It is the kind of agreement that Wittgenstein described in the *Philosophical Investigations* as agreement 'in the language we use' and as 'agreement in form of life'. Although, interestingly, in *On Certainty* he said of this last way of putting the point, about which so much has subsequently been written, that it is 'very badly expressed and probably very badly thought as well'.

The remarks on Frazer's *Golden Bough* help with this idea of agreement because of the light which they shed on the sense which Wittgenstein gave to the term 'primitive'. He maintained, for example, that Frazer's attempts to understand the magical and religious practices of primitive societies left no room for what I have just called a shared understanding which is not shared knowledge, or an agreement in judgments which is not an agreement about things which people either claim to know or think that they have good reasons for believing. Consequently, from Frazer's point of view, the only way in which one society might be said to be more primitive than another lay in the more or less adequate justifications which could be advanced for what they claimed to know. The less primitive, i.e. the more advanced, society will be one which can show how what were once thought to be good reasons must perforce give way to better. It was once thought that dancing might bring on the rain, but now we know better. Wittgenstein's remarks on *The Golden Bough*, all focused on the idea that this is the wrong way to seek to understand the religious and magical practices of 'primitive' societies.

> [O]ne might begin a book on anthropology in this way: When we watch the life and behaviour of men all over the earth we see that apart from what we might call animal activities, taking food, etc. etc. men also carry out actions that bear a peculiar

characteristic and might be called ritualistic./ But then it is nonsense if we go on to say that the characteristic feature of these
actions is that they spring from wrong ideas about the physics of
things. (This is what Frazer does when he says that magic is really
false physics, or as the case may be, false medicine, technology,
etc. (Wittgenstein, 1967, p. 33).

In other words, Wittgenstein's imagined book on anthropology,
would begin by stressing the central role of a particular way in
which human beings agree in what they say and do in any
endeavour to understand them in their different societies. What
I am maintaining is that such a book would bring to the forefront
of our attention that agreement which in the *Investigations* is said
to be necessary if language is to be a means of communication,
necessary, that is, for there to be societies at all.

On Certainty and the remarks on Frazer's *Golden Bough* help
to bring out that the agreement in judgments of *Philosophical
Investigations* 242 is a special kind of agreement. I am suggesting
that it is a central theme in Wittgenstein's later work, that it is
to this that we need to turn in our endeavours to get clear
about concepts. The introduction of the notion of agreement in
judgments is usefully thought of as a continued response to the
problem which made itself felt as a result of the depsychologising
of logic, and which had already exercised Wittgenstein in the
Tractatus. Proposition, thoughts, judgeable contents, sentences
in which something is said, divide into concepts. In order to
understand that division what we need is not a theory of language; a method of picking out, identifying or individuating the
parts into which they divide, and then a method of showing how
they fit together: rather what we need to do is to bring out the
way in which people agree in what they say, i.e. the way they
agree in the language they use.

The remark about agreement in judgments occurs at the
beginning of the celebrated passages in the *Philosophical Investigations* in which Wittgenstein considers the idea of a private
language, and it makes a great deal of difference to the way in
which we read these passages when we realise that the idea

under attack is the attempt to think of language divorced from the kind of agreement I have used *On Certainty* and the remarks on Frazer's *Golden Bough* to bring out. If, as I did a moment ago, we try to indicate the difference between the two sorts of agreement by thinking of one as a common understanding, and the other as common knowledge then we can begin to see that the idea of a private language that is being opposed is one which seeks to locate both our ability to say things, along with our ability to understand things said, in something that we know. The opposition is not so much between something only known to one person, and something known to everybody but between what we can be properly said to know and what we cannot. The idea that is being opposed is the idea that language can be developed and understood on the basis of what is known.

Recall Frege's remark with which I began this chapter to the effect that children do not learn to speak by building upon the linguistic knowledge which they already possess. In the same vein Wittgenstein argued that the development of a child's capacity to learn to speak is not constituted by the successive accumulation of more and more information. 'The child, I should like to say, learns to react in such-and-such a way; and in so reacting it doesn't so far know anything. Knowing only begins at a later level' (Wittgenstein, 1969b, p. 71).

To repeat, the idea that is being opposed is that language develops and is understood on the basis of what is known. The question of a private language i.e. a language in which the individual words 'refer to what can only be known to the person speaking' only arises when the resources of any knowledge other than private knowledge as the basis for learning a language have been shown to be inadequate. At that point the thesis that language develops on the basis of knowledge can only be safe-guarded by turning to some special knowledge, viz. private knowledge. The realm of private experience is the last resort for a theory that bases the development of a language along with the understanding of the nature of language, on things that can be known, i.e. about which truths can be discovered. The aim, and I think also the effect, of Wittgenstein's discussion of privacy was to show that this last resort is no resort at all.

One interesting consequence of this way of reading the relevant sections of the *Philosophical Investigations* is that, if it is correct, it shows how inappropriate is the suggestion by Saul Kripke, which seems to have been gaining ground in recent discussions, that Wittgenstein's grand strategy in that work was to develop a sceptical problem and provide a sceptical solution (Kripke, 1981). Kripke does indeed bring out well how no reference to what can be known about a person, whether it be oneself or another, will entail that a particular rule is being followed by that person. But it is quite wrong to present this as the development of a sceptical problem, that is to say, it is quite wrong to think of it as a problem about knowledge that needs to be resolved if scepticism about rule following is to be avoided. What it does show is that it is a mistake in the first place to treat the difficulties we have with regard to rule following as a problem of knowledge. To do so will be to remain at the level of agreement which takes disagreement as its contrast and to ignore what Wittgenstein wished to make central, viz. the way in which we agree in the language we use.

Having presented Wittgenstein as developing a sceptical problem about rule following, since Wittgenstein as the arch-sceptic strains credulity, Kripke is obliged to present what he takes to have been Wittgenstein's solution. He represents him as arguing in the following way. If no amount of knowledge that we can have of a person enables us to say of him that he is following a rule, in the use of a word, for example, i.e. if no amount of such knowledge enables us to understand what he means, or even that he means anything, then the only way forward is to sever the connection between meaning and truth which the concept of knowledge requires and to stress the connection between meaning and conditions of assertability. We get at the meaning of words not by considering the conditions under which what someone uses them to say is true, but by considering the conditions in which a person would be justified in using them in the way in which he does. While no knowledge of matters of fact about a person, psychological or otherwise, will enable us to conclude that a person is following a rule in the use of a word, nevertheless there are things that we can know about which will enable us to do this, viz. the conditions under which the community to which he belongs would consider itself justified in acknowledging that a rule was being followed.

The setting of Wittgenstein's discussion of privacy in the background of the problem of knowledge, or in the background of scepticism, requires, if we are not to be left with Wittgenstein the sceptic, that some knowledge be supplied which forms the basis of our ability to say whether a person is following a rule or not; forms the basis, that is, of our ability to say that he means something. The suggestion that Kripke foists upon Wittgenstein is that if we concentrate only on the person in question, even if that person happens to be oneself, we are left with the sceptical conclusion, but that if we broaden our horizons and take into consideration not only facts about that person but what we know about the community in which he lives, the sceptical conclusion is avoided. In the hypothetical case of a person actually in isolation, a Crusoe on a desert island before the advent of Friday, whether or not we can say of him that he follows a rule becomes the question of whether we can, in a manner of speaking, take him into our community and therefore utilise the knowledge we have of that to make judgments about him. Rule following presents a problem of knowledge only if we restrict our enquiries to a person considered entirely in isolation.

Whatever the merits this idea has in its own right, it clearly bears no resemblance to the stress which, I have argued, Wittgenstein places on the idea of agreement in judgments. For him, problems with regard to meaning are not considered either in the *Tractatus*, or in the *Philosophical Investigations* to be problems of knowledge at all. Problems about meaning, about following a rule, are conceptual problems, and concepts cannot be objects of knowledge.

The point can be illustrated by applying it to discussions of the concept of pain. If I say that I am in pain, and someone asks me how I know, what is it that he wants to know about? The situation would have to be extraordinary if what he wanted to know was whether I was in pain, since I have just told him that I am. Let us assume that it is not a question of him doubting my word. The question is only asked in the course of philosophical discussion, and what the philosopher wants to know about is not whether I am (really) in pain, but about the concept of pain. If I try to tell him about that by telling him what I know, then all the problems which beset Frege, and which led him to speak of a meeting of minds come flooding back in. The philosopher's problems, just because they are problems about concepts are not problems of knowledge, i.e. they are not problems which can be solved by finding out something which we previously did not know. About concepts there is no question of saying true (or false) things, and therefore our worries about them are not due to a lack of knowledge. Approaching Wittgenstein's work from the direction which led Frege to write about a meeting of minds helps to bring this point out.

It also helps with another term of art in Wittgenstein's writings, the term 'criterion'. When concepts prove troublesome, as for example, the concept of pain proves troublesome to the sceptical philosopher worried about 'other minds', Wittgenstein will remind us of the criteria associated with the concept that is giving the trouble. The reminders only have a point when our difficulties are conceptual difficulties. Apart from special circumstances we are not ordinarily troubled in the way in which the sceptic is about whether people are in pain or not. The sceptic is worried about whether anyone, (other than himself perhaps) is in pain. It is only with worries such as this that reminding us of the criteria for saying of someone that he is in pain has a point, for what we are being reminded of is the way in which we agree in the language we use when we say of someone that he is in pain. Once more, what we have learned from Frege about concepts, and what I have suggested we could have learned from Wittgenstein himself in the *Tractatus* if the temptation to read it through Russell's eyes had been resisted, affects the way in which we think of the business of adverting to criteria in the face of conceptual puzzlement. For there is a use of the term 'criterion' which is not like this at all. If we restrict ourselves to the situations in which we are genuinely worried about whether or not a person is in pain, e.g. the situation of a doctor wondering how one of his patients should be treated, then there are certain tests or observations that we shall make, which, if they turn out in a certain way, remove all doubt that the person is in pain. More generally, when we say of a particular subject that a predicate attaches to it we will do so after having measured it against the criteria for the predicate in question. Naturally there will be many areas in which we employ a term when we will be in some doubt about just what the criteria for its application are, and in many cases we shall have to make a decision. Nevertheless, the principle holds that we can move directly from the fulfilment of criteria in this sense, to the application of the term.

This is the sort of way which J.L. Austin used to invoke criteria in philosophy (Austin, 1961, p. 56). How do you know that it is a bullfinch? Consult the check-list of the characteristics of bullfinches. If the thing has those characteristics then there is no question that it is a bullfinch. An amateur ornithologist wondering whether a particular bird is a bullfinch needs to be informed by someone who knows just what those characteristics are. A person who needs to be told about criteria in this sense is not troubled about a concept in the way in which the sceptical philosopher is troubled about the concept of pain. The doctor wonders whether his patient is in pain, and the amateur ornithologist wonders whether the bird that he sees is a bullfinch. The doctor knows what tests to make (what the criteria are); he just needs to make them. The amateur ornithologist does not know what tests to make and needs some expert advice. The sceptical philosopher is in no such position. It is neither the case that he knows what tests to make but has not made them, nor is it the case that he does not know what tests to make and needs expert advice. Sceptical worries are conceptual worries, and worries about a concept cannot take the form of worries about a patient or worries about a bird or worries about any other thing. Concepts are not objects. The criteria that the sceptical philosopher needs to be reminded of, if he does need to be reminded of criteria, will not relate concepts to objects.

Now some philosophers have been tempted to ask at this point: 'If Wittgenstein's criteria do not relate concepts to objects then just what do they relate to what?' Do they perhaps relate concepts to concepts? This is the kind of question that Stanley Cavell asks in *The Claim of Reason*, where he answers it by saying that Wittgenstein's criteria 'do not relate a name to an object but various concepts to the concept of that object' (Cavell, 1979, p. 76). To ask such a question and to give such an answer is to be on the verge of losing the insight gained by setting Wittgenstein's discussion of agreement in judgments and therefore his use of the term 'criterion' in the background of Frege's discussion of concepts and objects. If we ask the question 'What do Wittgenstein's criteria relate to what?' even if we give the answer 'Not concepts to objects but concepts to concepts', we are nevertheless virtually forced to treat concepts as peculiar sorts of objects. Despite the considerable insight to be found in Cavell's discussion, (much of what I have said about Wittgenstein's use of the term 'criterion' has benefitted from reading his work), we can see that it does have this effect on him.

In discussing the difference between Austin and Wittgenstein in their use of the term 'criterion', Cavell distinguishes between what he calls 'specific objects' and what he calls 'generic objects'. Specific objects he describes as such that the problem of knowledge they present is one of 'correct description, identification or recognition', whereas generic objects 'are ones specifically about which there just is no problem of recognition or identification or description, ones about which the only problem, should it arise, would be not to say what they are but to say whether we can know that they exist, are real, are actually there.' He argues that Austin provided criteria when the knowledge in question is of a specific object, whereas Wittgenstein provided criteria when the knowledge in question is of a generic object. And so he writes:

> The general relation between these two notions of criteria is roughly this: If you do not know the criteria of an Austinian object (can't identify it, name it) then you lack a piece of information, a bit of knowledge, and you can be told its name, told what it is (officially) called. But if you do not know the criteria of Wittgensteinian objects then you lack, as it were, not only a piece of information or knowledge, but the possibility of acquiring information about such objects *uberhaupt*. You cannot be told the name of that object because there is as yet no object of that kind for you to attach a forthcoming name to. The possibility of finding out what it is officially called is not yet open to you (Cavell, 1979, p. 77).

In this passage Cavell is not just on the verge of misunderstanding the way in which Wittgenstein's invocation of criteria relates to his stress on the way in which we agree in the language we use, but well over the edge. To write in this way makes it look as though Wittgenstein only reminded us of criteria when the existence of some curious objects is at stake, perhaps 'mental objects' or for that matter 'physical objects'. With Frege in mind I think we can see better how the distinctions drawn in this passage reflect not a concern for the existence of particular kinds of objects but the crucial distinction between concepts and objects.

Although the passage with which the notion of agreement in judgment is introduced in the *Philosophical Investigations* makes no use of the term criterion at all, it should be clear, that the notion is playing a role there. If someone thought, for example, that we could explain what it is to measure something and then leave it as an open question whether people ever got the same results when they measured things; or if someone were worried by the absence of ways of arriving at an absolute precision in measurement and saw this as a reason for wondering whether any measuring had ever really been done, making it look as though what had up until now been called 'measuring' had really been something else, guessing perhaps, or estimating; then it would be proper to remind him of criteria for measuring, remind him that is that 'what we call measuring is partly determined by a constancy in the results of measurements'. If people did not, in the sense which I have been trying to bring out, agree in their judgments of measurement there would be nothing called measurement, no language of measurement, and therefore no scope for improving the standards of measurement, or for disagreements about whether any particular thing had been properly measured.

When we understand the difference between concepts and objects we realise that concepts, unlike objects, cannot be made the subjects of propositions. It follows from this that the upshot of conceptual investigations cannot be an accumulation of truths. If philosophical problems are conceptual problems then no accumulation of information is going to be of help with them. When criteria are invoked in cases where concepts prove troublesome they are not invoked as presenting the truth that will settle the issue. The conceptual confusion of which Wittgenstein wrote at the end of the *Philosophical Investigations*, when he said that in psychology there is experimental method and conceptual confusion, is not just muddled thinking, which might be due to ignorance or misinformation, or a lack of logical expertise. It is, as Frege recognised, a confusion founded on the nature of language. We mention an object when what we intend is a concept, and press for definitions when what we need to understand is a meeting of minds, or agreement in judgments, or the way in which we agree in the language we use. The kind of investigation which helps us to understand these things is what Wittgenstein called a grammatical investigation.

EIGHT

PRIVATE OBJECTS AND PUBLIC LANGUAGE

The various ways in which philosophers have sought to understand the unity of a proposition are reflected in their views of other matters. It could hardly be otherwise. It is likely to be agreed by all of the philosophers whom we have so far considered that philosophical investigations are conceptual investigations; the argument is only about what form such investigations can take. However, there is one area of perennial philosophical concern which is affected directly by what we say about concepts and objects. If the early doctrine of a third realm which is the concern of logic could have been sustained, then the conception of propositions and their unity would, arguably, have had no direct consequence with regard to philosophical considerations about the nature of the mind. On that account logical or philosophical investigations would be one thing, psychological investigations another. However, the problems that we have seen arise when we seek to understand propositions and their unity, when we seek, that is, to become clear about concepts, can scarcely leave that thesis untouched. If we need to appeal to, or be reminded of, the way in which we agree in the language we use in order to understand how something can be said, we at least have to regard human beings as agreeing in the language they use. Such a conception, at least on the face of it, rules out of court some influential accounts of the nature of human beings and the kind of understanding that we can have of them.

It seems to rule out of court, for example, the conception of the mind associated with Descartes. I say 'seems' just because some aspects of the Cartesian picture have remained attractive despite Ryle's polemic against the ghost in the machine and Wittgenstein's powerful arguments against the idea of a private language. I am not here going to rehearse those by now over-rehearsed arguments. Rather, in this and the following chapter, I want to show, in a more direct way, how two later influential attempts to save certain aspects of the Cartesian picture fail just because of a failure to understand the distinction between concepts and objects. They fail because they neglect the way in which we agree in the language we use.

In 1958 P.F. Strawson published what was to become an influential article entitled 'Persons'. He later incorporated a modified version of it as the central chapter of his book *Individuals*. Approaching it, as most philosophers did, from the background of the recently published work of Wittgenstein and Ryle, it seemed at first that its central thrust was the same. Like *The Concept of Mind*, 'Persons' held no brief for Cartesian egos, and like the *Philosophical Investigations* it stressed the public nature of our talk about the mind. 'One can ascribe states of consciousness to oneself' Strawson argued, 'only if one can ascribe them to others . . . and one cannot identify others if one can identify them *only* as possessors of states of consciousness' (Strawson, 1959, p. 100). On closer inspection, however, it turned out that this appearance was deceptive. The original article, although not the chapter in the book, made this clear from the beginning. It opened with a comment on a passage in the *Tractatus* in which Wittgenstein says 'The philosophical I is not the man, not the human body or the human soul of which psychology treats, but the metaphysical subject, the limit – not a part of the world.' As against this Strawson urged that:

> I do after all talk of that which has all of my experiences, I do talk of the subject of my experiences, – and yet of something that is part of the world in that it but not the world comes to a end when I die. . . . It may be difficult to explain the idea of something

that is both the subject of experiences and a part of the world. But it is an idea we have: it should be an idea that we can explain (Strawson, 1958, p. 127).

If we ask about those experiences which are my experiences it soon becomes clear that they are just those private experiences that Wittgenstein so powerfully argued against. What is special about the experiences of which I am the subject is just that, i.e. that I am the subject of them. They are my experiences in a sense of 'my' that entails that they cannot be anyone else's. Because no-one else can have them it follows that the basis for my knowledge of them in my own case is different from the basis of my knowledge of them in the case of others.

It becomes even clearer still when we consider Strawson's review of the *Philosophical Investigations*. In that review, after passages of high praise for Wittgenstein's elucidations of the concepts of meaning and understanding we find the following.

> Studying the sections in which Wittgenstein deals with sensations, one may well feel one's capacity to learn coming to an end. Wittgenstein's case against saying that the phrases 'meaning/understandng something by an expression' stand for or name special experiences seems to me to be thoroughly made out. But even the significance of this denial comes into question if it then appears that no word whatever stands for or names a special experience (Strawson, 1954, p. 41–42).

Strawson's article was, then, at least in part, a defence of the privacy of the mental. The problem, as he saw it, was to show how that thesis could be sustained without degenerating into a general scepticism or solipsism. He wanted to show how private states could be spoken of in a public language.

His defence of the privacy of the mental took the form of an argument to the effect that anyone who seeks to deny it is obliged to contradict himself. His strategy was first of all to characterise, in order to dismiss, a view, which he tentatively ascribed to Wittgenstein and Schlick, that states of mind are not owned at all and therefore not privately owned. Strawson thought that any philosopher who argues that in the use of first person psychological expressions the 'I' does not designate an owner or possessor must do so because such a philosopher must think that those who hold that it does, e.g. both Strawson himself and the defenders of Cartesian egos, are deploying an impermissible sense of ownership. What they seek to defend is a sense of ownership in which what is said to be owned is owned in a logically non-transferable way. They want a sense of 'mine' in which my experiences or my states of mind are mine in a way in which my house or my car is not. Descartes paradigmatically exemplified such a view. Recall that he arrived at a separate substance conception of mind as a result of the process of doubting. Ultimately for him I am what I cannot doubt myself to be; I am essentially what I cannot conceive of myself as not being. Descartes thought that while he could provide reasons for doubting that he had a body, he could provide no reason for doubting that he had states of mind or consciousness. He concluded, therefore, that while it was true that he had a body, his states of mind belonged to him in a sense different from that in which it was true to say that his body belonged to him. It is this sense of ownership, the sense that Strawson wished to defend, that the no-ownership proponents are supposed to consider to be illegitimate. They argue that there is no coherent sense of ownership in which what is owned is owned in a logically non-transferable way, and that therefore in the case of first person expressions the question of ownership does not arise.

Now Strawson took this idea to be equivalent to the view that what is said to have a state of mind is understood when the contingent dependency of such states on particular bodies is understood. He thought that if we did not accept such an equivalence the question of the identification of states of mind would at best have been side-stepped, and at worst have been rendered impossible to answer. Given this equivalence he argued for a strong sense of ownership on the grounds that such a view is incoherent.

It is not coherent, in that one who holds it is forced to make some use of that sense of possession of which he denies the existence, in presenting his case for the denial. When he tries to state the contingent fact, which he thinks gives rise to the illusion of the 'ego' he has to state it in some such form as 'All *my* experiences are had by (i.e. uniquely dependent upon the state of) body B'. For any attempt to eliminate the '*my*' or any expression with a similar possessive force would yield something that was not a contingent fact at all (Strawson, 1959, p. 96–97).

Since the attempt to identify states of mind by seeing them as contingently related to particular bodies cannot be coherently characterised it follows, Strawson thought, that if states of mind are to be capable of being identified at all, we need to retain the strong sense of ownership which so impressed Descartes, and which the no-ownership theorists seek to rule out. If Wittgenstein held that we must dispense with the notion of private objects since nothing can be said about them and 'nothing is as good as something about which nothing can be said', Strawson maintained that we must operate with the notion of private objects or we would not be able to identify states of mind and would therefore not be able to say anything about them. The problem that he thought needed to be solved was the problem of how we are able to say things about them given that they are in the required sense private. His question was 'What are the conditions which must hold for us to be able to speak as we do about private objects?'

Having developed the problem in this way Strawson's procedure was just to declare that in order to become clear about this we need to acknowledge what he calls the primitiveness of the concept of a person. We just have to accept that a person is something to which predicates of two radically different sorts can be predicated.

By predicates of radically different sorts he meant that one set cannot be reduced to the other even though the subject of the sets is the same in each case. The primitiveness of the concept of a person is constituted by the fact that a person is something to which both what he labelled 'P' (personal, psychological, private) predicates and what he labelled 'M' (material) predicates can be applied. If we acknowledge the primitiveness of the concept of a person our problem then becomes how that acknowledgement shows itself in our ability to deploy one of those sets of predicates, i.e. what it teaches us about the nature of the predicates in question. Descartes had said that a human being is such that these two sets of predicates can be applied to him because he is essentially two things, a mind and a body, so that while the body was the ultimate subject of one set the mind was the ultimate subject of the other. Strawson was prepared to conceive that the two sets of predicates are radically different, and on much the same ground as Descartes, but refused to condone a bifurcation of subjects. Once more, the refusal to accept such a bifurcation is just what the acknowledgement of the primitiveness of the concept of a person amounts to. Such primitiveness is not something which can be demonstrated; it has to be accepted.

In fact Strawson's view is in the end not so much different from the view which Descartes eventually arrived at. For Descartes too was obliged to conclude that 'I am not lodged in my body as a pilot is in a ship', which might be taken to imply that I am not 'lodged' in my body at all, and in a remarkable letter to Princess Elizabeth he suggested that whilst you can fnd out about the soul by 'metaphysical reflections which exercise the pure intellect' and find out about the body by the study of mathematics 'which chiefly exercises the imagination in considering figures and movements', it remained true that it was only by 'abstaining from meditating and from studying things that exercise the imagination that one learns to conceive of the union of soul and body' (Descartes, 1643, p. 280). This sounds very much like Descartes' way of saying that you just have to acknowledge that the two form a union and that the union that they form is not reducible to either.

What then, according to Strawson, do we learn about the language we use to speak of private experiences once we have acknowledged the primitiveness of the concept of a person? What we learn is that certain problems stem from a refusal or failure to make the acknowledgement. When I say of someone else that he is in pain or depressed, while the grounds that I have for saying this are different from the grounds that I have for saying the same thing of myself, as they would be if mine are to be mine in a logically non-transferable way, we would be refusing to acknowledge the primitiveness of the concept of a person if we concluded from this that therefore I do not really say the same thing of myself and the other person, or that I do not really know that the same thing is true of the other person as is true of myself. It belongs to the concept of a person that a person is such that the two sorts of predicates can be applied to him, and the fact that two sorts of predicates can be applied to him has implications with regard to what is meant by one of the sets of predicates. The fact that we can say of one and the same thing both that it weighs ten stones and that it is in pain is supposed to help us to understand how predicates of the first kind, M predicates, can be the basis of attribution of predicates of the second kind, P predicates. The fact that we can know of a person such facts as that he weighs ten stones as well as knowing of, let us say, a rock that it weighs ten stones, is meant to help us to understand how facts of that sort (although not, perhaps, this fact) can be the basis for the attribution of P predicates to him, even though they are not the basis for saying the same thing of oneself. A Cartesian ego would be beyond the knowledge of anyone other than that ego itelf, and therefore beyond the knowledge even of that ego, but a person is not beyond the knowledge of others since we do know that some people weigh ten stones. The fact that we are in a position to say things of that sort about a person other than oneself is, by itself, meant to show us that other subjects of P predicates are not necessarily opaque to us. And this in turn is meant to show us that there can be no logical bar to using physical characteristics, i.e. what we can know not only of persons but of things other than persons, as the basis of personal attributions. Acknowledging the primitiveness of the concept of a person is supposed to bring to our attention the logic of P predicates. It is supposed to alert us to the fact that they are predicates such that 'they are both self-ascribable otherwise than on the basis of the observation of the behaviour of the subject of them, and other-ascribable on the basis of behaviour criteria' (Strawson, 1959, p. 108).

Since there is no bar to using physical characteristics as the sole basis for that attribution of psychological predicates (once the primitiveness of the concept of a person has been acknowledged), the problem, Strawson thought, boils down to one of homing in on the relevant physical characteristics. While physical characteristics like weighing ten stones are not going to be of much help with regard to private experiences, there are other physical characteristics which might serve better. The most obvious of these, Strawson suggested, are the physical characteristics that are involved in the description of overt human behaviour. He therefore invited us to concentrate upon certain behavioural predicates (P predicates) in order to make clear how acknowledging the primitiveness of the concept of a person allows us to speak of private experiences in a public language. The predicates which he singles out for attention are predicates which imply both a state of mind and 'indicate a characteristic pattern, or range of patterns, of bodily movement while not indicating at all precisely any very definite sensation or experience' (Strawson, 1959, p. 111). The examples he gives are 'going for a walk', 'coiling a rope', 'playing ball', and 'writing a letter'.

Now what I think really impressed Strawson about these predicates is that while they are undoubtedly P predicates, i.e. they would be illegitimately predicated of anything other than persons, he thinks that they all entail predicates other than P predicates, viz. M predicates. The M predicates that they entail can therefore form the basis in knowledge for saying of others that the P predicate applies to them. The M predicates that such P predicates entail are all 'bodily movements' or 'patterns of bodily movements'. But since the P predicates in question are

ones which I know in my own case to apply not on the basis
of observation, I also know without observation that the M
predicates which they entail apply to me. It is because of this
that, in the case of others, those very M predicates which I can
observe to apply can be used as the basis for applying the P
predicates with which, in my own case, they are associated.
'Among the things that we observe', he wrote, 'as opposed to
the things we know about without observation, are the movements of bodies similar to those about which we have knowledge
not based on observation' (Strawson, 1959, p. 111–112). It is
this which is supposed to enable us to use certain physical
characteristics, which we can observe to hold of others, as 'criteria of a logically adequate kind' for the ascription of P predi
cates to them, just because they are the physical characteristics
involved in the P predicates which we know without observation
to apply to ourselves. We observe certain bodily movements but
we interpret them as actions.

Acknowledging the primitiveness of the concept of a person
is thus supposed to enable us to see, what otherwise would be
unintelligible, how psychological predicates, while not reducible
to physical predicates can nevertheless be applied to others on
the basis of physical predicates. If we generalise the argument
we arrive at the required conclusion that the acknowledgement
of the primitiveness of the concept of a person enables us to
speak of private objects in a public language. The language is
founded on the individuation of physical items. A logical non-
transferable sense of ownership permits the individuation of
psychological states, but it is the association of psychological
states so individuated with observable physical states that
enables there to be a public language about them.

Philosophers later began to point out, although not generally
in connection with Strawson's views, that this way of thinking
about the way in which we speak about both our states of mind
and the states of mind of others is really grotesque. In an
impressive paper called 'Human Beings', J. W. Cook recalls a
remark of F. Ebersole to the effect that philosophers often speak

of people as if they were speaking of zombies, corpses which are somehow made to move as though they were alive (Cook, 1969, p. 125). This was, indeed, the way in which Strawson was constrained to think and speak about other people. All we actually observe are certain physical movements which we interpret as behaviour.

If you actually try to think of yourself as doing this with regard to the people around you, you begin to see immediately what an extraordinary picture it is. Ebersole himself in his book *Things we Know* shows by a series of what I can only describe as devastating examples that the attempt to understand human behaviour by beginning with something which is not human behaviour, but, as the older psychologists used to say, 'mere bodily movements' ('colourless movements' as Hull had it), and interpreting them by setting them in a particular background is hopeless (Ebersole, 1967, p. 291). For many years such a view was widely held, and not just in circles that might be called behaviourist. After the onslaught on the Cartesian picture of the mind, philosophers, over-impressed, perhaps, by the gains to be had by game comparisons, and in particular the game of chess, argued that what needed to be done was to set bodily movements (Strawson's M predicates) in a rule-governed social background. Just as the mere movement of a piece of wood of a certain shape is supposed to become a move in chess only when seen in the background of the rules of chess so, it was argued, the mere bodily movements of human beings only become human behaviour when seen in the background of the rules of society. A. I. Meldon's book *Free Action* was perhaps the most influential work in this respect. In it he described children as being trained 'to recognise *this* bodily movement of its mother in *this* transaction in which it engages, as *this* action, *that*, bodily movement in *that* transaction as *that* action', and he encouraged us to explore 'the various ways in which social and moral institutions, conventions, statutes etc., are relevant to the background activities against which bodily movements are understood as the actions they are' (Meldon, 1961, p. 190).

It should be clear, however, that setting colourless movements, even of a human body, in the background of the rules and conventions of society could not possibly have the effect of turning them into anything that could be called human behaviour. The model does, indeed, as Ebersole pointed out, provide us with a way of understanding how something which is already an human action can have a different force, or become quite a different action, if set in different backgrounds: raising one's hand in a lecture is to do something different from raising one's hand while sitting in a motor car at the start of a Grand Prix, just because raising one's hand is already to do something. But a model which serves well to explain how one action becomes another, or how one action takes on a different force, will be a non-starter when used to explain how something which is not an action but a mere bodily movement becomes one.

However, the reason why I have chosen to discuss Strawson's views about the language we use to speak about states of mind is not just because I consider them to be mistaken, but because I think that the way in which Strawson arrived at these views brings out clearly how the views he held about the nature of the mind arose from views he held about the nature of concepts.

Strawson arrived at the idea of private states spoken of in a public language because the problems with which he began were problems of individuation. The philosophical tradition in which he wrote is the long search for a principle of individuation. This search is relevant to our concerns just in so far as we have already seen the idea of such a principle at work in the attempts to break a proposition into parts, i.e. in the attempt to find a principle of individuation for parts of propositions. Moreover we have also seen how such an attempt fails. Concepts are not individuals, not even individuals in a third realm. That of course might still leave untouched individuals in the other two realms, i.e individuals in the realm of body and in the realm of mind, and the search for a principle of individuation in those two realms could still go on. In a certain sense, the assertion of the privacy of states of mind is just the assertion that there is a principle of individuation for states of mind. There is a parallel privacy claimed for bodies within the tradition of the search for a principle of individuation. The capacity which a body has to occupy space to the exclusion of all other bodies might well be called the privacy of bodies, the space which they occupy is private to them. As two bodies cannot share the same space at the same time, so can nobody else have my states of mind. And just as this fact, if it is a fact, about bodies is not one, *pace* Locke, which observation reveals, but belongs to our conception of body, the solidity which bodies possess is, so to speak a logical solidity: neither is the fact of the privacy of mental states, if it is a fact, a fact which observation reveals. Both are requirements of the thesis that at the heart of our ability to say things about minds and bodies there lies the idea of a principle of individuation for mental items and physical items. What I am suggesting is that this thesis, in its turn, is a version of a more general thesis that at the heart of our ability to say anything at all there lies the question of individuation, and that this must reflect itself in the view we take about the way in which our sayings are constituted. We have in other words returned to an itemising account of propositions. The second part of *Individuals* is best construed as a defence of just such a view, the aim of which is to overcome the problems which Frege (and, as I have argued, Wittgenstein) thought it generated and which, as I have also shown, led the former to speak of a meeting of minds and the latter of agreement in judgments.

When we read the second part of Strawson's *Individuals* with this in mind, it is remarkable how closely his views in that part of the book resemble the views of Russell in part one of *The Principles of Mathematics*. Recall, once more, how Russell introduced a technical sense of 'denoting' in order to explain how something which is eternally a term, a logical subject, can appear in a proposition other than as a term. Commenting on his own discussion of Frege's distinction between concept and object Strawson told us that the main thing that he wanted to establish is that what is valuable in Frege's work is that it brings to our attention the need to draw:

> an absolute distinction between two mutually exclusive classes of expressions, members of each of which can combine with suitable members of the other to yield an assertion. Members of the two classes of expressions alike introduce terms; but the members of one class introduce them assertively, and the members of the other class do not .... Essentially the distinction we have arrived at is a distinction between styles of introduction of terms (Strawson, 1959, p. 154).

While the details of Strawson's view about the nature of a proposition differ from Russell's, both held tight to the view that a proposition needs to be thought of as having constituents that can be made into logical subjects, for that is what for both Strawson and Russell terms are. We have already seen this to be true of Russell in chapter two, but it is equally true of Strawson.

If we take 'logical subject' to mean what a proposition is about, then, Strawson argued, a proposition such as 'Raleigh smokes' could, depending upon the context, be said to be either about Raleigh or about smoking. Each of these, he maintained, is suitably thought of as a logical subject. The expression 'Raleigh' in 'Raleigh smokes' serves to introduce the particular person Raleigh and the expression 'smokes' serves to introduce the habit, smoking. 'Let us say', Strawson wrote, 'that anything which is introduced, or can be introduced, into a remark by an expression is a *term*.' Moreover, just as Russell insisted that while terms which appear as terms in propositions are named, and terms which appear in propositions not as terms are denoted, and that naming and denoting are radically different, so Strawson insisted on two radically different kinds of term introduction: the introduction of terms in the referring style and the introduction of terms in the assertive style.

Holding tight to Russell's way of thinking about propositions he was, needless to say, confronted with the problems which led

Russell to his theory of the variable, and which led Frege to the metaphors of unsaturatedness and incompleteness. His response to these problems will bring us back to what I have described as the grotesque picture of how we think of other people as having states of mind, which will bring out how it derived from his way of thinking about the language we use to speak of states of mind.

The conception of propositions as made up of terms and the sentences expressing them as introducing them in various ways, requires that terms be capable of identification. 'The term-introducing expression' Strawson argued, 'indicates, or is meant to indicate, what term is introduced by its means' (Strawson, 1959, p. 154). What he proposed was that it is the way in which identification is effected that requires that there be two quite different styles of term introduction, and at the same time explains why Frege was right to insist that concept-introducing expressions are incomplete in a way in which object-introducing expressions are not.

If an expression has to have the job of introducing an object into our discourse, Strawson insisted, then not only must there be an object for the expression to introduce, but there also must be some means of identifying and re-identifying the object in question. We need to know what object we are talking about. It follows from this, he maintained, that there must be some fact about the object in question, known to the speaker, which will serve to distinguish it from any other object. It is this which accounts for the sense of completeness of object-introducing expressions. They are complete in the sense that a condition for them doing the job they are designed to do is that something is true of the object they serve to introduce. However, although questions of identification do indeed arise with concept-introducing terms, the identification in this case is not effected by means of the knowledge of any fact. If, for example, the expression 'Socrates' in 'Socrates is wise' introduced the term Socrates, this is so because the person who uses it knows something about Socrates which distinguishes him from any other thing. However, the expression 'wise' in the same sentence introduces its term without there being any such corresponding fact. The person who uses it does not need to know that any particular person is wise or that any person at all is wise. But still the doctrine of term introduction requires that he know something, i.e. the term that is introduced stands in need of identification. The person introducing it by means of the expression 'wise' needs to know what wisdom is. Knowing what wisdom is, however, unlike knowing who Socrates is, is not to be appraised of a fact but to have knowledge of the language of which the expression 'wise' is a part. The difference between knowledge of a particular fact and knowledge of the language of which an expression is a part, accounts for the sense of completeness which is associated with object-introducing expressions and the sense of incompleteness associated with concept-introducing expressions.

Objects, then, according to Strawson, are identified by knowledge of matters of fact and concepts are identified by knowledge of language. In both cases what is known serves the purpose of identification. What I am suggesting is that it is this idea of what saying something is which ultimately generated the picture of how we say things about states of mind which I have characterised as grotesque. It forced Strawson to provide an answer to the question 'What must we know about the language in which we speak of states of mind which enables us to identify the terms that are introduced by expressions for those states of mind?' This is the sense in which he asked for the criteria that we employ in saying of someone that he is in pain or depressed etc.

In the sentence 'John is in pain' we are introduced both to the object John, and to the concept pain. We must therefore know something which uniquely identifies John and we must know something about the language which enables us to identify the concept pain. Part of what we know that uniquely identifies John is that he is a person, i.e. that he is something to which two radically different kinds of predicates can be appropriately predicated, and that one of these kinds includes the predicate

' . . . is in pain'. This is something that we just have to acknow-ledge. It belongs to the idea of the primitiveness of the concept of a person. But, equally, part of what we know about the language of which the expression 'pain' is a part, is that ' . . . is in pain' can be predicated of persons other than oneself, and that therefore the knowledge that we can have of another person must be capable of providing adequate grounds for saying of him that he is in pain. If we assume, as Strawson did, that our knowledge of others is based upon observation, and assume as well, again as Strawson did, that all that can be observed in the case of others are their bodily movements then we are in a position to say what we know about a language containing the expression 'pain' which enables us to introduce a term by means of it. What we know is that it belongs to what we mean by 'pain' that knowledge of bodily movements gives us adequate grounds for employing the term with regard to others. It is in this way that a view about the constituents of propositions, i.e. Strawson's doctrine of 'terms' and 'term introduction', generated a view about the nature of the mind which when taken seriously pre-sents a grotesque picture of the way in which we stand to other people.

If we did not have enough reason to drop the doctrine of terms, the theory of mind which Strawson argued it generates would be an added inducement. By showing how the doctrine generates such a theory we can see more clearly the consequences of trying to understand the nature of language by concentrating on what we can be said to know, and the damage that is done when in the philosophy of mind we neglect the way in which we agree in the language we use.

NINE

THE NEW WAY OF IDEAS

The second example that I wish to examine of how mistaken views about concepts generate mistaken views about the nature of the mind requires that we go back to the very beginning. I argued in chapter one that the changed conception of logic at the turn of the century originated in the depsychologising of logic which was brought about by the work of Bradley and Frege. In recent years a version of that psychology, although not always recognised as such, has begun once more to dominate writings on the philosophy of mind. I am referring to the development of a new cognitivism bolstered by the power that is claimed for the techniques of computer simulation to solve philosophical problems about the nature of the mind now widely held by workers in the field of 'artificial intelligence'. Daniel Dennett, for example, commenting on the tendency of workers in that field to refer to what they are doing as 'experimental epistemology' thinks that while 'such a characterisation is liable to "make a philosopher's blood boil" . . . if AI called itself instead thought-experimental epistemology philosophers ought to be reassured' (Dennett, 1978, p. 117). Dennett is only one of a growing number of philosophers who have come to think that research in the discipline that has become known as 'artificial intelligence', together with allied work in linguistics, provides a basis for a new philosophy of mind. In point of fact, however, the philosophy of mind for which it provides a basis is not new at all. Just as Chomsky in linguistics readily admits that the conception of language he advocates bears a strong resemblance to conceptions of language influenced by Descartes' conception of the mind, so the view of the mind associated with the idea of artificial intelligence is Descartes'. Both in linguistics and in the philosophy of mind an old conception has been revived by the introduction of computational tools and techniques.

It is worthwhile reminding ourselves of some of the most familiar passages in the writings of Descartes to bring out just how closely they are related to the views now espoused by modern defenders of cognitivism in general and by devotees of artificial intelligence in particular.

Perhaps the first statement of the view is to be found in Descartes' *Rules for the Direction of the Mind*

> The cognitive power is always one and the same: if it applies itself along with the imagination, to the common sensibility, it is said to see, feel, etc.; if it applies itself to the imagination alone, in so far as that is already provided with various images, it is said to remember; if it does this to form new images, it is said to imagine or conceive; if, finally, it acts by itself, it is said to understand. . . . In accordance with these diverse functions the same power is now called pure intellect, now imagination, now memory, now sense; and it is properly called mind when it is either forming new ideas in the phantasy or attending to those already formed (Descartes, 1701, p. 170).

It must be remembered when reading this that for Descartes in this work both the imagination and the common sensibility are thought to be bodily. We get a conception of the psychological or the mental when we conjoin such physical apparatus with a uniform faculty, i.e. a power of knowing or understanding. This is how the old 'way of ideas' began.

Even when the theory was first introduced one of its benefits was thought to be that it provided an explanation of the nature of the language. In the *Discourse on Method*, for example, Descartes claimed that 'if there were machines resembling our bodies, and imitating our actions as far as is morally possible', we should still be able to tell that they were not really men for they 'could never use words or other constructed signs, as we do to declare our thoughts to others.' Such a machine would lack the ability to 'arrange words variously in response to the meaning of what is said in its presence' (Descartes, 1637, p. 41–42). The reason why Descartes thought that machines could never do this is that, from his point of view, they would of necessity lack the power of forming 'ideas' i.e. they would lack a cognitive power which is the same wherever it is found. In short they would lack the ability to represent things for themselves. The power of representing things to ourselves both enables knowledge to be gained, famously for example in *Meditation Two* that this object is a piece of wax, for the 'perception of the wax is not sight nor touch nor imagination' but 'a purely mental contemplation', and at the same time enables us to use language to express the knowledge we have.

The advantages of the 'old way of ideas' are difficult to over-estimate. Not only did the doctrine free philosophy from the literal unintelligibility of the version of scholastic philosophy that was then being taught (for example to Descartes himself at *La Flèche*) with its substantial forms and intentional forms, or 'little jumping forms', as Descartes himself caricatured them. It also introduced an admirable egalitarianism into conceptions of human beings. For since the 'cognitive power is always one and the same' it follows that 'good sense is the most evenly distributed thing in the world'. However the doctrine as well as generating epistemological problems which philosophers subsequently struggled to overcome, and which still form the basis of many university courses in epistemology, had at its centre what seemed until the advent of the computer a fatal flaw, first brought to light by Hume.

The postulation of 'ideas' by means of which we not only gain knowledge of things but also by means of which we are able to express that knowledge requires a conception of someone who uses them. It requires, as Hume noticed, a conception of a self. Yet the doctrine that knowledge is mediated by 'ideas' which requires a conception of the self also entails that the self is something of which we can have no knowledge. Hume notoriously acknowledged that this was a problem he could not solve.

> For my part, when I enter most intimately into what I call *myself*, I always stumble on some particular perception or other, of light or shade, love or hatred, pain or pleasure. I never catch myself at any time without a perception, and never observe anything but a perception ... If anyone upon serious and unprejudic'd reflection, thinks he has a different notion of *himself*, I must confess that I can no longer reason with him (Hume, 1739, p. 252).

It is this problem which researchers in artificial intelligence claim to have solved and thus to have begun to rehabilitate cognitivism. A new 'way of ideas' which utilises the techniques of computer simulation is now seen by many as a means of making inroads into philosophical problems in general and problems about the nature of minds in particular. In short, it threatens to eliminate the gains for our understanding of philosophical or logical investigations which originated in the depsychologising of the subject by Bradley and Frege. Daniel Dennett's paper 'Artificial Intelligence as Philosophy and as Psychology' in *Brainstorms* is generally thought to provide a clear statement of the rationale for this development.

The problem with 'ideas' which Hume was the first to expose, seems to deal a death blow to any conception of the mind based upon the attribution of internal representations, for that, as we have seen from Descartes, is just what 'ideas' are. If we have no clear account of a user or interpreter of representations, then to think in terms of representations being internal, i.e. to think in terms of 'ideas' merely pushes the problem further back. Dennett set up the problem in the following way.

> [S]omething is only a representation for or to someone; any representation or system of representations thus requires at least one *user* or *interpreter* of the representation who is external to it. Any such interpreter must have a variety of psychological or intentional traits: it must be capable of a variety of *comprehension* and must have beliefs and goals (so it can *use* the representation to *inform* itself and thus assist itself in achieving its goals). Such

an interpreter is therefore a sort of homunculus (Dennett, 1978, p. 122).

The postulation of internal representations in psychology requires us to think in terms of an homunculus, (Ryle's 'ghost in the machine'), which in turn would have to be thought of as operating with internal representations requiring the postulation of a further homunculus and so on *ad infinitum*. Dennett acknowledged the 'so on' but thought that computer simulation could remove the *ad infinitum*.

He first of all pointed out that while homunculus talk is very widespread amongst workers in 'artificial intelligence', far from it being harmful there, it turns out to be extremely beneficial. The reason for this, he thought, is that homunculi are not invoked to explain abilities wholesale. It is this which eventually enables a theory of internal representations to halt the infinite regress which threatens its intelligibility. 'If one can get a team or committee of relatively ignorant, narrow minded, blind homunculi to produce the intelligent behaviour of the whole, this is progress.' The way in which the progress is made is illustrated by the example of a flow chart.

A flow chart is typically the organisation chart of a committee of homunculi (investigators, librarians, accountants, executives); each box specifies a homunculus by prescribing a function *without* saying how it is to be accomplished (one says in effect: put a little man in there to do the job). If we then look closer at the individual boxes we see that the function of each is accomplished by subdividing it via another flow chart into still smaller, more stupid homunculi. Eventually this nesting of boxes within boxes lands you with homunculi so stupid (all they have to do is to remember to say yes or no when asked) that they can be, as one says 'replaced by a machine'. One discharges *fancy* homunculi from one's scheme by organising armies of idiots to do the work (Dennett, 1978, p. 123–124).

Offered this as a solution to Hume's problem one wonders how it could ever have been thought to be one, for it is clear that Hume's problem remains even at the level of the stupidest homunculus. Hume's problem really does require that homunculi are dispensed with altogether, otherwise the nature of 'ideas' or internal representations will remain as obscure as ever. But Dennett's homunculi, however stupid, are still the sort of thing which can be called stupid, and it is mere evasion just to add that they can be 'as one says "replaced by a machine".' Not only have they to be able to say something but they also have to be able to remember to say something, even if what they have to be able to say and to remember to say is not very much. It is altogether inconceivable how the notion of an internal representation can be explained by an invocation of the ability to say something, however little. Descartes, as we have seen, worked the theory the other way round, invoking internal representations to explain our ability to say things, but at least he had the excuse that he had no Hume to point out the difficulties in that account.

Moreover, there is more than a slight resemblance between the technique which Dennett used to overcome the 'ghost in the machine' regress and the solution which Descartes himself adopted with regard to a problem about the relation of mind and body which his own views generated. Recall his suggestion that the mind only acted on a very little part of the body, the pineal gland, as though the problem of mind body interaction, inherent in the idea that mind and body are separate substances, could be solved by making the part of the body on which the mind is supposed to act as small as possible. And just as for Descartes the interaction of the mind with however small a part of the body has the effect of destroying completely the doctrine for which the pineal gland was meant to provide the solution, so for Dennett the invocation of an interpreter or user of representations, however meagre the representations such as interpreter is said to be able to employ, has the effect of destroying completely the idea that we have a method at our disposal for utilising internal representations while dispensing with homunculi.

Hume's problem can be thought of as a problem about the nature of intentionality. If we characterise the problem in a linguistic mode we can say that one criterion of an intentional verb is that propositions containing it do not retain their truth value through changes in 'correct characterisations of their objects. They do not go through the logical hoops of what P.T. Geach calls 'Shakespearian inference' (Geach, 1963, p. 139). While that which we call a rose by any other name would smell as sweet, what we think about, worship or intend would not necessarily be thought about or worshipped or intended if its characterisation were altered even to something which is true of what we think about worship or intend. Oedipus thought about Jocasta and intended to marry her, and it is true that Jocasta was his mother, but it by no means follows that Oedipus thought about his mother and intended to marry her. With regard to intentional verbs the characterisation of the object is, as G.E.M. Anscombe has pointed out, all-important (Anscombe, 1965, p. 161). In the case of the example that I have given this point could be expressed in a non-linguistic way by saying that what someone intends or what someone thinks about carries with it implications about how what is thought about or intended is represented to the person who does the thinking or intending. Problems about intentionality and problems about representation are not independent problems. Hume's difficulties over a self which has 'ideas' dramatically illustrate this. 'Ideas' or internal representations are not something capable of independent specification followed by subsequent allocation to users. They are what they are because of the way in which they are used. If we seek to discharge the user and, as they say, replace him by a machine then we will simultaneously deprive ourselves of representations or 'ideas'. The idea of employing theoretical homunculi while progressively restricting their jobs may have much to teach us, but it will not solve Hume's problem.

Before trying to show in more detail why this is so and how it relates to difficulties over the nature of concepts, it is worthwhile considering a prior question. How, given that

Dennett's solution to Hume's problem is manifestly no solution, could it possibly have been thought to be so? I think that part of the answer to this question is that Dennett's solution is a solution to a problem which looks like Hume's problem but really is not. If states of mind are, as a matter of fact, just brain states then we know in advance of producing a solution that Hume's problem can be solved. One way of understanding the thesis of the contingent identity of mind and body is to think of it as just being the thesis that there are no logical problems with regard to that identification; that is what makes the thesis of identity a thesis of *contingent* identity. Moreover, if the identity thesis is stated in a particular way an added impetus is given to the deployment of intentional notions once we are assured that they can ultimately be dispensed with. If we express the purported identity of states of mind with brain states by saying (a) 'For any person there are brain states that are identical with states of mind' rather than by saying (b) 'There are brain states that for any person are identical with states of mind', then the possibility is left open that such brain states may differ from person to person, and indeed that they may be different in the same person at different times. If such were the case then the kind of approach that workers in 'artificial intelligence' advocate would be eminently sensible. If there are indeed no logical problems in dispensing with intentionality then we can construct something which looks like Hume's problem and set out to solve it by computational means. We set ourselves the problem of how a large-scale human ability whose characterisation would involve representational or intentional characterisations could be the consequence of a series of smaller scale abilities whose description would also involve intentional or representational characteristics, and then ask about these smaller scale abilities the same question, and so on. The aim in the end will be to arrive at a point when no further possible subdivision can be made. We then add the reminder that we know in advance that there is no logical reason why the having of such abilities will not turn out to be identical with having our brain in a particular state. When that point is reached, the computational or top-down approach will have come into contact with the physiological or bottom-up approach. However, the whole programme, far from solving Hume's problem, requires that the problem has already been solved in advance by the mind-brain identity thesis. It requires that we know that there is nothing objectionable in the supposition that states of mind are states of brain.

Although it would take me too far from my immediate concerns to confront directly the thesis of contingent identity which in recent years has rapidly assumed the status of a dogma, since I am using Dennett to illustrate the new 'way of ideas' it is perhaps worthwhile pointing out that his version of the identity thesis is particularly dangerous. Using the idea that problems about intentionality, or problems about the nature of representation, have already been in principle solved, Dennett argued that we can be quite safe in our philosophical *cum* psychological research if we utilise the power of our ordinary intentional concepts by moulding them into a system. We can then use such a system not only in the explanation of human behaviour but also to understand the way in which we understand our ordinary psychological concepts. A systematised version of belief, desire, intention, etc. will help us to understand those concepts themselves. 'Every mental event' he argued 'is some functional physical event or other, and the types are captured ... by a regimentation of the very terms we *ordinarily* use – we explain *what beliefs are* by systematizing the notion of a believing system' (Dennett, 1978, p. xix). When, however, our ordinary psychological concepts prove recalcitrant to such systematisation, as they invariably do, Dennett argued that far from this providing a reason for questioning the systematising endeavour, we should rather conclude that there is something wrong with what we are trying to understand! It should come as no surprise to us, he claimed, that 'most of our familiar mentalistic idioms fail to perform the task of perspicuous reference, because they embody conceptual infelicities and incoherences of various sorts' (Dennett, 1978, p. xix).

Let us now turn to the question of why Hume's problem is not capable of solution by computational means. My suggestion here hinges on the terminology with which Dennett began, i.e. the idea that the work done in artificial intelligence can be correctly characterised, or is best thought of, as conducting thought experiments. The view is that while the phrase 'experimental epistemology' smacks of confusion, the confusion of supposing that epistemological problems can be solved by empirical means, if we can envisage a form of experimentation that is not empirical then the possibility of an experimental epistemology opens up. It is here that the notion of thought experiments comes into play. Thought experiments are experiments all right, but they are precisely not empirical experiments. They are experiments which deal not so much with what is the case but with what might be the case; not with actualities but with possibilities. Possibilities may be unactualised, but what is actual has at least to be possible. *Ab esse ad posse valet consequentia.* What lies at the heart of Dennett's way of thinking, and is, I think, at the heart of the conviction that work in artificial intelligence constitutes a gain in philosophical understanding, is the idea that the techniques of computer simulation have at last provided philosophers with a way of systematically exploring possibilities. In other words it is claimed that the discipline of the computer enables us to turn our *a priori* speculations into genuine thought experiments; computation standing to speculation about possibilities in the way in which experimentation stands to speculation about actualities. Computers, as they are utilised in work in artificial intelligence, should, on this account, be thought of as the 'prosthetic regulators' of our *a priori* speculation.

With such a characterisation of thought experiments we can return to Hume's problem. We have seen how that problem turns out to be insoluble even by prosthetically regulated thought experiments. While Hume's problem is correctly thought of as a problem about the possibility of a psychology which utilises a notion of internal representations ('ideas'), such a possibility is not one which is capable of being explored in a prosthetically regulated way. This is not to say that many of the problems which Hume tackles are not such that thought experimentation would be inappropriate. It is often fruitful to ask ourselves how it is possible for us to think of the world in the way in which we do. We speak of the world, for example, in terms of cause and effect, and if we are convinced that in order for one event to be the effect of a prior event it must be necessarily connected with that prior event, and we are equally convinced that we do not have observational access to necessary connections between events, it clearly makes sense to experiment in thought and ask ourselves how our talk about cause and effect is possible. We know that Hume's answer to this question, as to a variety of other questions, was to refer us to the role of the passions in human affairs. It may even be true (although I very much doubt it) that his speculations about such a possibility could have benefitted from modern means of prosthetic regulation. But the situation is not like this when in the Appendix to the *Treatise* the problem of the self is raised, and it is to Hume's credit that he realised this was so. The question, as he raised it, about cause and effect does indeed require us to experiment in thought, but the question of the Appendix does not. It raises quite a different problem about 'ideas', or in modern terminology, internal representations.

What I am suggesting is that Hume's problem about the self which has ideas is one version of the problem of the unity of a judgment, or the unity of a proposition which has been my central concern in this book. As soon as you conceive of judgments or propositions as consisting of items of whatever sort, the question becomes one of explaining how the unity of what is judged or proposed can be maintained. In the case of Hume it is not just that he flounders with regard to the question of the self, and can come up with no satisfactory conclusion, but rather that the very idea of a self which has 'ideas' only comes into question because 'ideas' are thought of in the way in which they are. When Locke, for example, wrote that personal identity is dependent upon the consciousness which accompanies all perceptions 'it being impossible for anyone to see, feel, etc. without at the same time perceiving that he does see feel etc.' we will miss the point if we suppose that all that is at stake is that our states of mind are self-intimating or refulgent. The important point is not so much that states of mind illuminate themselves, even though they were supposed to possess this property, but that rather they intimate not only themselves but the self which has them. It is in that sense that states of mind are self-revealing. They need to be, for without a self that has them they are not in themselves anything to be revealed. If it is true, as Hume urged, that 'no proposition can be intelligible or consistent with regard to objects which is not so with regard to perceptions' or 'ideas', then we do require some principle which holds ideas together. If we think of the components of thoughts as mental objects then we need an answer to the question 'What makes just those objects into this thought?' What makes the 'idea' of Socrates and the 'idea' of wisdom into the thought that Socrates is wise? Within the 'way of ideas' the traditional answer was that they are turned into a judgment by a self thinking them together. Those mental items which are 'ideas' are turned into judgments and not just bundles by the self thinking them together. What Hume came to admit was that from within the 'way of ideas' we can make neither head nor tail of such a conception of the self. Earlier in the *Treatise* he had been bold enough to suggest that the self was nothing but a bundle of perceptions (impressions and 'ideas'). In the Appendix we find the honest recognition that such a conception would prevent the self from even being that, for without the notion of a self the job that impressions and ideas were imported to perform could not be performed by them. Without a self impressions and 'ideas' are nothing, and yet with 'ideas' and 'impressions' the self cannot be made intelligible.

The moral to be drawn from the difficulties with the 'way of ideas' that Hume brought to light is the moral that in fact Bradley did draw when he said that 'the image of psychological idea is for logic nothing but sensible reality.' If we think of 'ideas' in connection with meaning, which we clearly do when we move into the modern terminology of internal representations, then such an 'idea', taken by itself 'is an adjective divorced, a parasite cut loose, a spirit without a body seeking rest in another, an abstraction from the concrete, a mere possibility which by itself is nothing' (Bradley, 1883, p. 8). Logic, in other words can have nothing to do with internal representations psychologically conceived, i.e. conceived of as psychological entities, or for that matter as entities of any sort.

I have already tried to show in chapter three how the founder of modern logic, Frege, became increasingly aware as his views developed that the main source of contamination of what he called the logical source of knowledge was 'the tendency to form proper names to which no objects correspond', i.e. a tendency to treat concepts as objects. He thought that the difficulties in which this tendency entangles us are incalculable. I have also argued in chapter four that it was this realisation which lay behind Wittgenstein's 'In a manner of speaking, objects are colourless' of the *Tractatus*. It also, I think lay behind his rejection in the *Philosophical Investigations* of the picture of language in which 'every word has a meaning. This meaning is correlated with the word, it is the object for which the word stands'. Cartesian and Lockean 'ideas' together with the internal representations of the new cognitivism are just such objects. Bradley and Frege were the first to realise that 'ideas' so conceived were irrelevant to logic. It was to be another half century before it was being proclaimed that they are not relevant to any subject whatsoever: that, as Ryle so vividly put it, they belong to the myth of the ghost in the machine. It is an historical accident that the development of philosophy from Bradley to Ryle coincided with the development in psychology of various forms of behaviourism. These were much more influenced by the

failures of introspectionist psychology, and a hankering for the
measurable than by any considerations of logic or of the nature
of logical investigations. It is sheer confusion to place *The Concept
of Mind* (and even worse Wittgenstein's *Philosophical Investigations*) within that tradition, and see it as reinforcing a form
of materialism by providing a behaviouristic interpretation of
mental concepts. Ryle certainly did reject the 'way of ideas',
and we have seen in chapter five the conception of philosophical
investigations which lay behind the rejection of it. 'Ideas', he
argued 'belong where "phlogiston" belongs and where "substantial forms" belong, namely the folk-lore of philosophy'. Yet
he found its defenders more worthy opponents than the adher-
ents of the materialism which it replaced. 'The Cartesian myth'
he wrote, 'does indeed repair the defects of the Hobbist myth
only by duplicating it. But even doctrinal homeopathy involves
the recognition of disorders' (Ryle, 1938, p. 330). And yet it is
this alternation, either behaviourism or a psychology which
utilises 'ideas' (or internal representations) which is the largest
single impetus behind the current resurrection of cognitivism.
Ryle would have urged, indeed he did urge, that this dichotomy,
like most logicians' dichotomies, needs to be taken with a pinch
of salt.

Hume's problem was a problem about the nature of concepts.
It arises when we seek to identify concepts with one special kind
of item. Hume thought of concepts as a special kind of object,
but realised in the end that if we think of them in that way it
becomes impossible to see how they could play the role that they
are invoked to play. How could objects give us the way in which
we represent objects (the world) to ourselves? It is this problem
which generated the infinitely regressive search for a super-
object, the self, which would serve to turn inner-objects into
genuine representations, i.e. to find a part of the world that
would explain how we can think about the world. It should now
be clear that there is no part of the world that could do such a job.
This is what I suggest gives force to the remark in Wittgenstein's
Tractatus that 'The philosophical I is not the man, not the human

body or the human soul of which psychology treats, but the metaphysical subject, the limit – not part of the world.' Within the old 'way of ideas' the self which has 'ideas', the self which is intimated by any 'idea', was a requirement of 'ideas' doing the job they were invented to perform, that of being representations of the world. Much of the work in artificial intelligence is founded on the view that we will one day discover that some part or parts of the world are capable of doing the same job, and that we now have the tools, computers, to find them; a view bolstered by the belief that when they are found we should not be surprised if they turn out to be identical with something physical. Frege's reflections on the distinction between concepts and objects should persuade us that the goal is quite literally inconceivable. They also, I think, serve to illuminate the celebrated remark at the end of Wittgenstein's *Philosophical Investigations* in which he compared work in psychology to work in mathematics.

> The confusion and barrenness of psychology is not to be explained by calling it a 'young science'; its state is not comparable with that of physics for instance, in its beginnings. (Rather with certain branches of mathematics. Set theory.) For in psychology there are experimental methods and *conceptual confusion*. (As in the other case conceptual confusion and methods of proof) (Wittgenstein, 1953, p. 232).

Defenders of the new cognitivism in general and practitioners in the field of artificial intelligence in particular are inclined to write as though psychology, with the aid of computers has finally come of age, and that the prosthetic regulation of computer simulation has finally given us the means whereby we can avoid the conceptual confusion of earlier generations to which Wittgenstein was supposedly referring. With Frege's distinction in mind we should rather conclude that they themselves provide us with a perfect exemplification of that very confusion. The conceptual confusion that the *Philosophical Investigations* brings to light is in the end best thought of as a confusion about the nature of concepts. In mathematics there is an inclination to confuse concepts with sets or classes, and this is an example of the same sort of error that Hume and Descartes made when they thought of concepts as mental objects. It is the sort of error which the new 'way of ideas' perpetuates.

BIBLIOGRAPHY OF WORKS CITED

The date of original publication is given first followed by reference to the edition used, together with its date when this is not the same as the original.

Anscombe, G. E. M. 1965, 'The Intentionality of Sensations', in *Analytic Philosophy*, Second Series, ed. R.J. Butler, Oxford, Blackwell.

Anscombe, G. E. M. and Geach, P.T. 1954, *Descartes' Philosophical Writings*, London, Nelson.

Austin, J. L. 1961, 'Other Minds', in *Collected Philosophical Papers*, Oxford, Clarendon Press.

Ayer, A.J. 1971, *Russell and Moore: The Analytic Heritage*, London, Macmillan.

Bradley, F. H. 1883, *The Principles of Logic*, Second Edition, Corrected Impression, Oxford, University Press, 1928.

Bradley, F. H. 1893, *Appearance and Reality*, Second Edition, Oxford, Clarendon Press, 1930.

Cavell, S. 1979, *The Claim of Reason*, Oxford, Clarendon Press.

Cook, J. W. 1969, 'Human Beings', in *Studies in the Philosophy of Wittgenstein*, ed. P. Winch, London, Routledge & Kegan Paul.

Davidson, D. 1967, 'Truth and Meaning', in Davidson, 1984.

Davidson, D. 1969, 'True to Facts', in Davidson, 1984.

Davidson, D. 1977, 'Reality Without Reference', in Davidson, 1984.

Davidson, D. 1984, *Inquiries into Truth and Interpretation*, Oxford, Clarendon Press.

Dennett, D. 1978, *Brainstorms*, Sussex, Harvester Press, 1979.

Descartes, R. 1637, *Discourse on Method*, in Anscombe and Geach, 1954.

Descartes, R. 1643, 'Letter to Elizabeth', in Anscombe and Geach, 1954.

Descartes, R. 1701, *Rules for the Direction of the Mind*, in Anscombe and Geach, 1954.

Dummett, M. 1973, *Frege, Philosophy of Language*, Second Edition, London, Duckworth, 1981.

Ebersole, F. 1967, *Things we Know*, Eugene, Oregon.

Frege, G. 1879, *Begriffschrift*, in Geach and Black, 1952.

Frege, G. 1884, *The Foundations of Arithmetic*, trans. by J. L. Austin, Oxford, Blackwell, 1950.

Frege, G. 1892, 'On Concept and Object', in Geach and Black, 1952.

Frege, G. 1904, 'What is a Function?' in Geach and Black, 1952.

Frege, G. 1912, in *From Frege to Godel. A Source Book in Mathematical Logic*, ed. J. van Heijenoort, Cambridge Mass, 1967.

Frege, G. 1918, 'The Thought: A logical Inquiry' Trans. A. and M. Quinton, in *Mind* vol. LXV, 1956.

Frege, G. 1969, *Posthumous Writings*, Trans. P. Long and R. White, Oxford, Blackwell, 1979.

Geach, P. T. and Black, M. 1952, *Translations from the Philosophical Writings of Gottlob Frege*, Oxford, Blackwell.

Geach, P. T. 1963, 'Quantification Theory and the Problem of Identifying Objects of Reference', in *Logic Matters*, Berkeley and Los Angeles, University of California Press, 1972.

Hacker, P. M. S. 1975, 'Laying the Ghost of the *Tractatus*' in *Review of Metaphysics*, Vol. 29.

Hume, D. 1739, *A Treatise of Human Nature*, ed. Selby Bigge, Oxford, Clarendon Press, 1888.

Kenny, A. 1973, *Wittgenstein*, London, Allen Lane the Penguin Press.

Kenny, A. 1974. 'The Ghost of the *Tractatus*', in *Understanding Wittgenstein: Royal Institute of Philosophy Lectures*, Vol. 7, ed. G. N. A. Vesey, London, Macmillan.

Kripke, S. 1981, 'Wittgenstein on Rules and Private Language', in *Perspectives on the Philosophy of Wittgenstein*, ed. I. Block, Oxford, Blackwell.

Meldon, A. I. 1961, *Free Action*, London, Routledge & Kegan Paul.

Mill, J. S. 1843, *A System of Logic*, Peoples Edition, London, Longman and Co., 1891.

Moore, G. E. 1899, 'The Nature of Judgment', in *Mind*. Vol. viii.

Pears, D. F. 1971, *Wittgenstein*, London, Fontana/Collins.

Pears, D. F. 1977, 'The Relation Between Wittgenstein's Picture Theory of Propositions and Russell's Theory of Judgment', in *Philosophical Review*, Vol. 86.

Russell, B. 1903, *The Principles of Mathematics*, Second Edition, London, Allen and Unwin, 1937.

Russell, B. 1905, 'On Denoting', in *Readings in Semantics*, eds. F. Zabee, E. D. Klemke and A. Jacobson, University of Illinois Press, Chicago, 1974.

Ryle, G. 1932, 'Systematically Misleading Expressions', in Ryle, 1971b.

Ryle, G. 1935, 'Internal Relations', in Ryle, 1971b.

Ryle, G,. 1938, 'Categories', in Ryle, 1971b.

Ryle, G. 1945, 'Philosophical Arguments', in Ryle, 1971b.

Ryle, G. 1949, *The Concept of Mind*, London, Hutchinson.

Ryle, G. 1953, *Dilemmas*, Cambridge, University Press.

Ryle, G. 1956, *The Revolution in Philosophy*, London, Macmillan.

Ryle, G. 1957, 'The Theory of Meaning', in Ryle, 1971b.

Ryle, G. 1960, 'Letters and Syllables in Plato', in Ryle, 1971a.

Ryle, G. 1962, 'Phenomenology Versus the Concept of the Mind', in Ryle, 1971a.

Ryle, G. 1970, 'Autobiographical', in *Ryle*, ed. O. P. Wood and G. Pitcher, Anchor books and Doubleday.

Ryle, G. 1971a, *Collected Papers* Vol. 1, London, Hutchinson.

Ryle, G. 1971b, *Collected Papers* Vol. 2, London, Hutchinson.

Strawson, P. F. 1954, Review of Wittgenstein's *Philosophical Investigations*, in *Wittgenstein*, ed. G. Pitcher, London, Macmillan, 1966.

Strawson, P. F. 1958, 'Persons', in *The Philosophy of Mind*, ed. V. C. Chappell, Englewood Cliffs, N. J., 1962.

Strawson, P. F. 1959, *Individuals*, University Paperback Series, London, Methuen, 1964.

142   BIBLIOGRAPHY OF WORKS CITED

Urmson, J. O. 1956, *Philosophical Analysis*, Oxford, Clarendon Press.

Wittgenstein, L. 1921, *Tractatus Logico Philosophicus*, Trans D. F. Pears and B. F. McGuiness, London, Routledge & Kegan Paul, 1961.

Wittgenstein, L. 1953, *Philosophical Investigations*, Second Edition, Oxford, Blackwell, 1958.

Wittgenstein, L. 1967, 'Remarks on Frazer's *Golden Bough* in *The Human World*, No. 3, 1971.

Wittgenstein, L. 1969a, *1914–16 Notebooks*, ed. G. H. Von Wright and G. E. M. Anscombe, Oxford, Blackwell.

Wittgenstein, L. 1969b, *On Certainty*, Oxford, Blackwell.

INDEX